······· The Formatting Toolbar

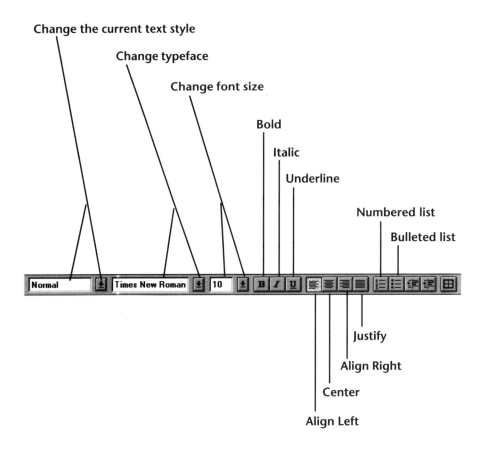

For every kind of computer user, there is a SYBEX book.

All computer users learn in their own way. Some need straightforward and methodical explanations. Others are just too busy for this approach. But no matter what camp you fall into, SYBEX has a book that can help you get the most out of your computer and computer software while learning at your own pace.

Beginners generally want to start at the beginning. The **ABC's** series, with its step-by-step lessons in plain language, helps you build basic skills quickly. Or you might try our **Quick & Easy** series, the friendly, full-color guide.

The **Mastering** and **Understanding** series will tell you everything you need to know about a subject. They're perfect for intermediate and advanced computer users, yet they don't make the mistake of leaving beginners behind.

If you're a busy person and are already comfortable with computers, you can choose from two SYBEX series—**Up & Running** and **Running Start**. The **Up & Running** series gets you started in just 20 lessons. Or you can get two books in one, a step-by-step tutorial and an alphabetical reference, with our **Running Start** series.

Everyone who uses computer software can also use a computer software reference. SYBEX offers the gamut—from portable **Instant References** to comprehensive **Encyclopedias**, **Desktop References**, and **Bibles**.

SYBEX even offers special titles on subjects that don't neatly fit a category—like **Tips & Tricks**, the **Shareware Treasure Chests**, and a wide range of books for Macintosh computers and software.

SYBEX books are written by authors who are expert in their subjects. In fact, many make their living as professionals, consultants or teachers in the field of computer software. And their manuscripts are thoroughly reviewed by our technical and editorial staff for accuracy and ease-of-use.

So when you want answers about computers or any popular software package, just help yourself to SYBEX.

For a complete catalog of our publications, please write:

SYBEX Inc.
2021 Challenger Drive
Alameda, CA 94501
Tel: (510) 523-8233/(800) 227-2346 Telex: 336311
SYBEX Fax: (510) 523-2373

SYBEX is committed to using natural resources wisely to preserve and improve our environment. As a leader in the computer book publishing industry, we are aware that over 40% of America's solid waste is paper. This is why we have been printing the text of books like this one on recycled paper since 1982.

This year our use of recycled paper will result in the saving of more than 15,300 trees. We will lower air pollution effluents by 54,000 pounds, save 6,300,000 gallons of water, and reduce landfill by 2,700 cubic yards.

In choosing a SYBEX book you are not only making a choice for the best in skills and information, you are also choosing to enhance the quality of life for all of us.

Up and *Running*

with Word 6 for Windows™

Rita Belserene

SYBEX®

San Francisco • Paris • Düsseldorf • Soest

Acquisitions Editor: Joanne Cuthbertson
Developmental Editor: Sarah Wadsworth
Editor: Peter Weverka
Project Editor: Abby Azrael
Technical Editor: Elizabeth Shannon
Chapter Artist: Lisa Jaffe
Screen Graphics: John Corrigan
Typesetter: Thomas Goudie
Proofreader/Production Assistant: Sarah Lemas
Indexer: Ted Laux
Cover Designer: Archer Design
Cover Illustrator: Richard Miller

Library of Congress Card Number: 93-86590
ISBN: 0-7821-1421-0

Manufactured in the United States of America
10 9 8 7 6 5 4 3 2 1

· · · **Acknowledgments**

I would like to thank the many people who provided support and assistance throughout the writing of this book.

I am especially grateful to Peter Weverka, whose capable editing makes this a much more useful and readable text. He was able to help enormously with the difficult task of keeping this volume short and clear.

I would also like to thank Joanne Cuthbertson, Sarah Wadsworth, Abby Azrael, and Elizabeth Shannon at SYBEX. Each of them helped keep this project on track.

On a personal note, I would like to thank Heidi Dorsey. Her caring and capable attention to my son Joe gave me the hours needed to complete this project. Finally, as always, I want to thank my husband Don, who helps our household stay afloat when his wife tries to juggle one task too many.

$\cdots$ Table of Contents

· · · Introduction

Microsoft Word has enjoyed increasing popularity because it is one of the most flexible, easy-to-use word processing programs available. With the release of Word 6.0 for Windows, many new features have been added that make Word even more powerful and easy to work with. This book covers all the basics you'll need to get started with Word 6.0 for windows.

· · · How This Book Is Organized

The concise, carefully organized steps in this book are designed to help you get comfortable with Word right away. Steps 1 through 6 cover the basics you'll need to know for any kind of work you do with Word. The remaining steps cover one or more additional features that you can use as you feel the need. These steps are designed to stand alone so that you can read them in any order or refer to them to get precisely the kind of information you need.

Each step is designed to give you quick and clear instructions. A *fast track* at the beginning of each step gives a concise summary of key material that follows. For many tasks, the fast tracks will be all you need to read. The illustrations in each step show you the screen displays you'll be working with and include lots of helpful information. In the text you'll find step-by-step instructions, tips, and warnings that help you work more efficiently.

Tips are marked with this icon in the margin. Tips give you information for making your work easier.

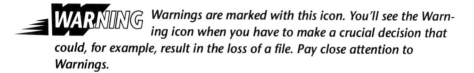 Warnings are marked with this icon. You'll see the Warning icon when you have to make a crucial decision that could, for example, result in the loss of a file. Pay close attention to Warnings.

 Notes tell you where you can go elsewhere in the book for more information.

 When you are asked to perform a specific action, you will see the Action icon.

· · · Mouse and Keyboard Instructions

All Word commands can be given using either the keyboard or mouse. Although both mouse and keyboard techniques are included in this book, mouse commands are given most often. (This helps keep instructions clear and straightforward. You'll probably want to experiment to see whether using the mouse or keyboard suits you best.)

The ➤ symbol appears when you are given a series of menu- selection instructions. For example, instead of telling you to "open the File menu and select New," you will see the following instruction:

Select File ➤ New.

Mouse Terminology

In order to understand the directions given in this book, you will need to know the following terms for working with your mouse:

TERM	MEANING
Mouse pointer	The small arrow that moves on screen as you move the mouse on your desk.
Insertion point	The vertical line that shows you where your text will be inserted when you press a key.
Click	Press and release the mouse button once. If no button is specified, use the *left* mouse button.
Double-click	Click twice in rapid succession.
Drag	Click and hold down the mouse button. While you hold the button down, move the mouse pointer to a new location on screen.

• • • Function Keys

For giving keyboard commands, you should be familiar with the *function keys* on your keyboard. These are usually arranged across the top of the keyboard, and are labeled F1, F2, and so on. Many keyboard commands involve using two (or three) keys together. These are shown with a plus sign (+). You needn't try to land on these keys simultaneously. For example, to give the command Alt+F4, hold down the key labeled Alt, and then press the F4 function key.

• • • **Exploring Further**

Word 6.0 is an enormous and complex program. No book this size could possibly cover all of its features. The material presented here is designed to get you started as quickly and painlessly as possible. Once you've worked your way through the steps in this book, you'll probably feel comfortable enough with the program to explore many more features on your own. As you do, you can take advantage of Word's extensive built-in Help system. The Help features are covered in Step 7. Let this book get you "up and running" with Word, and then use the Help system to explore the wealth of more advanced features that Word offers.

The Basics:
Starting and Exiting

● ● ● ● ● ● *f a s t   t r a c k*

To start Word, double-click the Microsoft Word icon in the Microsoft Office group window.

Word displays a "Tip of the Day" message when you start up. Click OK to close this message.

To exit from Word, open the File menu and select Exit (or press Alt+F4).

IN this step, you'll learn what every Word user needs to know—how to start and exit the program. This step also explains the the Quick Preview screen and "Tip of the Day" messages.

 *If you are unfamiliar with terms such as "double-click" and "Alt+F4," read the Introduction before continuing. The Introduction also explains how to use your mouse and keyboard.*

••• Starting Word

To start Word, Windows should be running on your computer, and the Microsoft Office group window should be open. Figure 1.1 shows this window. (Your desktop will look different.) If your Microsoft window is not open and you need to open it:

- Find the icon labeled Microsoft Office and double-click on it.

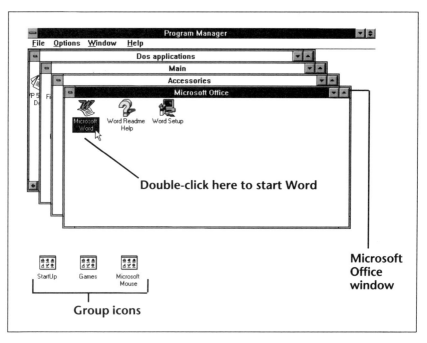

FIGURE 1.1: *The Windows desktop and the Microsoft Office window*

To start Word:

- Double-click on the icon labeled Microsoft Word in the Microsoft Office window.

After a moment, a Word document window will appear.

> **TIP** *If you recently installed Word, you will see the Quick Preview screen the first few times you start the program. Click Getting Started to see a Quick Preview demonstration. Click Return to Word to close the Preview screen.*

Tip of the Day Messages

When Word is first installed, it automatically displays a "Tip of the Day" message each time you start up. Read these messages to learn more about Word. Click OK to close the Tip of the Day message. If you don't want to see these messages each time you start Word:

- Click to remove the *X* in the box labeled Show Tips at Startup.

When the program is loaded (and you have cleared the Quick Preview screen and the Tip of the Day message if they were displayed), you should see a Word document window.

··· Exiting from Word

Always exit from both Word and Windows before turning off your computer. To exit from Word, use one of these techniques:

- Select File ➤ Exit.
- Double-click on the Word Control button (Control buttons are explained in Step 2).
- Click on the Word Control button and select Close from the Control menu.

- Press Alt+F4

What happens next depends on whether you made changes to the document before you exited Word:

- If you made no changes to the document, you will be returned to the Windows Program Manager.

- If you altered the document screen, Word displays a dialog box asking if you want to save your work.

 *For now, click No (or press N) to return to the Program manager. (Saving documents is covered in Step 3.)*

To exit from Windows:

1. Double-click on the Program Manager Control button (in the upper-left corner of the desktop), or press Alt+F4.

2. Click OK in the Exit Windows dialog box.

Getting Acquainted with Word for Windows

To give a menu command, click on a menu name and then click on the command you want.

To open a shortcut menu, move the mouse pointer to an on-screen item with a shortcut menu and click the *right* mouse button.

To activate a toolbar button, click on it.

IN this step, you'll learn the fundamental skills you need to work with Word for Windows. This step explains the document window, how to give commands, how to use the shortcut menus and toolbars, how dialog boxes work, and how to change the appearance of the screen to suit your work habits.

··· The Document Window

The Word document window is where you create and edit documents. Figure 2.1 shows what this window looks like when you first run Word. Important parts of the window are labeled.

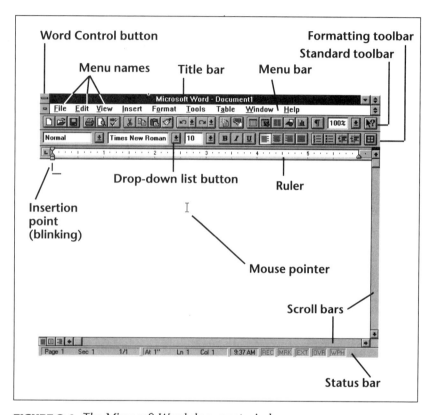

FIGURE 2.1: *The Microsoft Word document window*

··· Giving Commands

There are several ways to give Word commands. You can use the menus, the shortcut menus, or the toolbars. Spend some

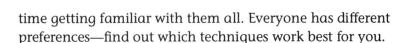

time getting familiar with them all. Everyone has different preferences—find out which techniques work best for you.

Using the Menus

You can accomplish any task in Word by using the *pull-down menus.* Figure 2.2 shows an open, or pulled-down, menu.

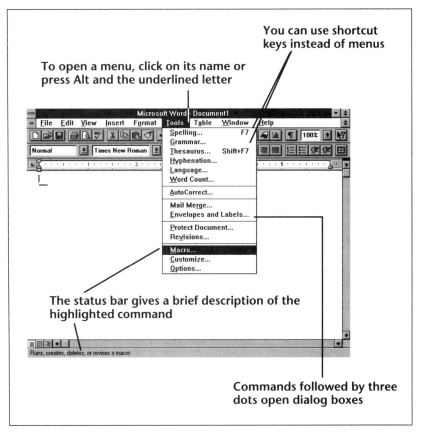

FIGURE 2.2: *A Word pull-down menu*

Menu names are displayed in the *menu bar* at the top of the document window. To display the list of commands under a menu name:

- Click on the menu name with your mouse, or
- Hold down the Alt key and press the underlined letter in the menu name. For example, press Alt+F to open the File menu.

TIP *When a menu is open, Word displays a brief description of the highlighted command in the status bar at the bottom of the screen. Press ↑ and ↓ to highlight different commands and see what they are used for.*

To select a command on a menu:

- Click on the command name, or
- Press the underlined letter in the command name.

TIP *Notice the keystroke combinations, called* shortcut *keys, next to some command names. You can press a shortcut key to give a command immediately and not have to open any menus.*

To close an open menu:

- Click in the document window, outside the menu; or
- Press the Esc key twice.

The Shortcut Menus

You can access Word's most commonly used features with the *shortcut menus*. Figure 2.3 shows the Toolbar shortcut menu. Shortcut menus are also available for paragraph formatting, tables, graphics, and other advanced features. These menus give you quicker access to Word commands than the menus at the top of the screen do.

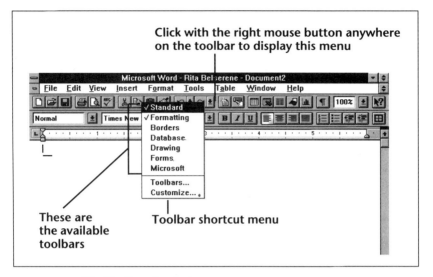

FIGURE 2.3: *The Toolbar shortcut menu*

To display a shortcut menu:

1. Place the mouse pointer on a part of your screen that provides a shortcut menu. For example, you could place the mouse pointer on the toolbar.

2. Click the *right* mouse button.

Which shortcut menu you see depends on where your mouse pointer was located when you clicked the right mouse button.

Once the menu is displayed, choose a command as you would on any other menu.

You can display some shortcut menus with the keyboard. For example, to display the Paragraph formatting menu, either click the right mouse button in the document window or press Shift+F10.

Using the Toolbars

For quick access to the most frequently used commands, take advantage of Word's Standard and Formatting *toolbars*. (They are labeled in Figure 2.1.)

Toolbars include *buttons* and *drop-down* lists.

- Click on a button to access the command it represents.

- Where you see a ↓ on a toolbar, it means that clicking on the arrow displays a drop-down list of options. Click on the arrow, and then click on the option you want.

 *To find out what an item on a toolbar does, just move the mouse pointer to the item. Word will display its name after a short pause.*

 *The inside-front cover of this book show the names of tools on the toolbars.*

· · · **How Dialog Boxes Work**

Some commands are not executed immediately. When Word needs to get more information from you to complete a command, it displays a *dialog box*. Figure 2.4 shows a sample dialog box and describes techniques for working with dialog boxes.

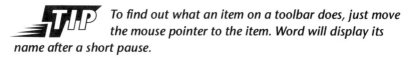 *Menu commands that open dialog boxes are followed by three dots (...).*

Try opening some dialog boxes to get a feel for what they look like. Click the Cancel button (or press Esc) to close the open dialog boxes. You'll learn about individual dialog boxes throughout this book.

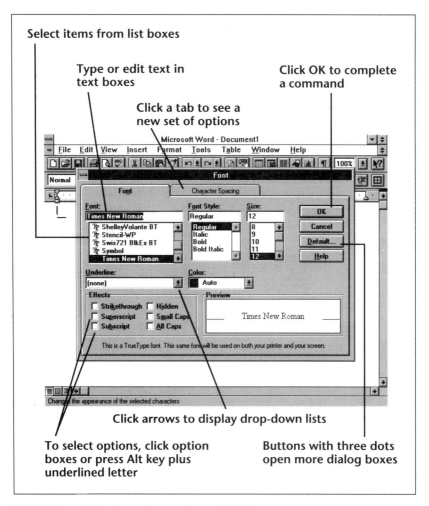

FIGURE 2.4: *Techniques for working with dialog boxes*

••• Changing the Screen Display

You can change the appearance of your Word screen to suit your tastes:

- To clear the editing tools from the screen so you can see more of your document, choose View ➤ Full screen. To return to the original display, either click on the Full Screen icon that appears or press the Esc key.

- To turn parts of the screen display on and off, use the View menu. For example, to remove the ruler, select View ➤ Ruler. To display the ruler again, repeat the same steps.

- To add or display different toolbars, choose View ➤ Toolbars and place an X next to the toolbars you want to display.

Creating, Saving, and Retrieving Documents

To create a document, simply type in the document window. Let Word begin new lines where appropriate.

To save a document, click the Save button in the toolbar (or press Ctrl+S).

To open a new document, click the New button on the toolbar.

To retrieve a document you have saved, click the Open button on the toolbar (or press Ctrl+O).

IN this step, you'll learn how to create a document, how to save it, and how to retrieve documents you have saved. This step also explains word wrapping and non-printing characters.

···**Creating a Document**

To create a document:

- Type your text with the keyboard. As you type along, try pressing the Backspace key. This key erases the last character you typed. Pressing Del erases the next character.

 *Step 4 explains more techniques for erasing and making changes in a document.*

Word Wrap

With an electric typewriter, you must press the Return key at the end of each line of text to begin typing the next line. With Word, however, you let the program arrange text for you. When you reach the end of a line, Word automatically begins the next line for you. This is called *word wrap*. Word wrap makes typing faster and easier.

TIP *Use word wrap if you plan to make changes to what you have typed. If you let Word arrange your lines when you first type them, they will be rearranged automatically whenever you add or take out words later on.*

At times you won't want to use word wrap. For example, when you reach the end of a paragraph or type a short line of text, such as a title or the salutation in a letter, you press the Enter key to end the line. (The Enter key is labeled ↵ on some keyboards.)

Printing and Non-Printing Characters

The letters, numbers, and symbols on the keyboard are examples of *printing* characters. These characters appear on screen the same way they will appear on paper when you print the document. However, some keys—including Enter, Tab, and the Spacebar—insert *non-printing* characters in the document.

Word lets you view non-printing characters on screen so that you can see, for example, where you entered a tab space or a new paragraph in your document. Each non-printing character is represented by a symbol. Figure 3.1 shows a sample document with the non-printing character display turned on.

To turn the non-printing character display on or off:

- Click the ¶ toolbar button (this button is identified in Figure 3.1).

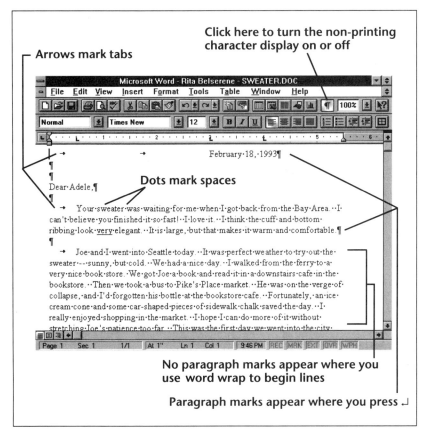

FIGURE 3.1: *Displaying non-printing characters*

••• Saving a Document

The text you type on screen is stored in your computer's electronic memory. However, until you *save* your document, the text you type is considered "temporary" text. When you save the document, Word transfers an electronic copy of the text to your hard disk. Only saved documents can be retrieved again later.

 *Save your document frequently as you work. This helps ensure that you will be able to retrieve it easily, even if something unexpected—such as a power failure—occurs.*

Saving a File for the First Time

Use one of these techniques to save a document:

- Click the Save button on the toolbar.
- Press Ctrl+S.
- Select File ➤ Save.

In order to save a document, Word needs a *file name* to store it under. When you give the Save command for the first time, Word displays the Save As dialog box shown in Figure 3.2. This is where you enter a name for your new file.

1. Enter a name in the File Name text box. Use eight letters or fewer. Don't add your own file extension, as Word automatically adds a three letter *.doc* extension to the file name.

2. Click OK.

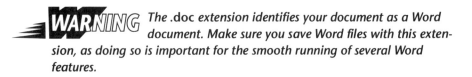 *The .doc extension identifies your document as a Word document. Make sure you save Word files with this extension, as doing so is important for the smooth running of several Word features.*

Click here to save a file

Word saves your file to this directory

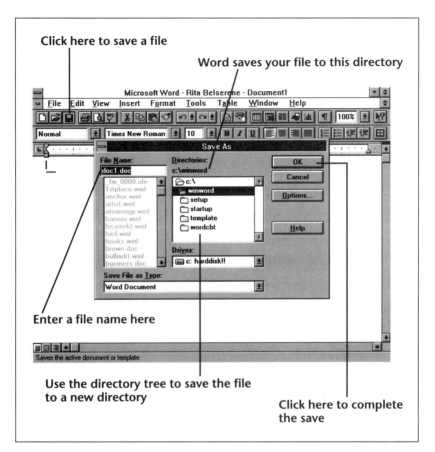

Enter a file name here

Use the directory tree to save the file to a new directory

Click here to complete the save

FIGURE 3.2: *The Save As dialog box*

After you save a file, Word displays its name in the title bar of the document screen.

 *If you don't enter a file name, Word provides a name for you, such as* doc1.doc, doc2.doc, *and so on.*

Word stores document files in the same directory as your Word program files unless you tell it to do otherwise. To store files in an organized fashion, you should create directories for storing your document files. See Step 19 for information.

Saving a File That Has Already Been Named and Saved

To save a file that has already been named and saved, use one of these techniques:

- Click the Save button on the toolbar.
- Press Ctrl+S.
- Select File ➤ Save.

Word simply saves the changes without reopening the Save As dialog box.

If you want to save a changed version of a file under a new name and keep the original version as well, use the Save As command in the File menu (not the Save command). Word will reopen the Save As dialog box. Enter your new file name.

• • • Opening a Clear Document Screen

To open a new, clear screen when you already have a document on screen:

- Click the New button on the far left of the Standard toolbar.

Your first document will disappear from the screen but remain *active* so you can bring it up again quickly. When you exit the program, Word closes all active documents and gives you a chance to save any unsaved work.

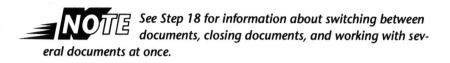 *See Step 18 for information about switching between documents, closing documents, and working with several documents at once.*

• • • Retrieving a Document

You can open documents directly from the File menu or use the Open Document dialog box. Each method is explained below.

Retrieving Files Quickly with the File Menu

When you open the File menu, the four files you worked with most recently are listed at the bottom, as shown in Figure 3.3. To open one of the four files:

- Click on the file name, or
- Press the number next to the name.

Retrieving Files with the Open Command

To retrieve any file on disk, use the Open dialog box shown in Figure 3.4.

1. To display the Open dialog box, use one of these methods:

- Click the Open button in the toolbar (see Figure 3.4).
- Press Ctrl+O.
- Select File ➤ Open.

Files with the *.doc* extension appear in the list box under the File Name text box. (You can use the List Files of Type scroll box to list files with extensions other than *.doc*. If you've

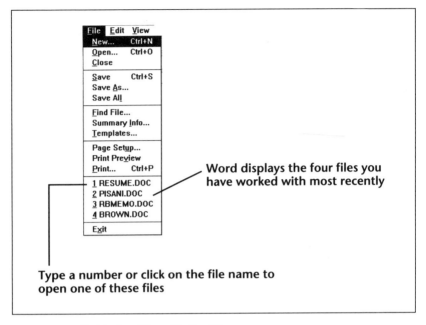

Word displays the four files you have worked with most recently

Type a number or click on the file name to open one of these files

FIGURE 3.3: *Retrieving files with the File menu*

chosen to display other types of files with this scroll box, *.doc* files will not appear in the list box under File Name.)

2. To identify the file you want to open:

- Type the file name directly into the File Name text box, or

- Click on the file name in the list box below it.

3. Click OK.

 To open a file quickly, double-click on its name in the Open dialog box.

 *Directories are explained in Step 19.*

Files listed are located in this directory

Click here to display the Open dialog box

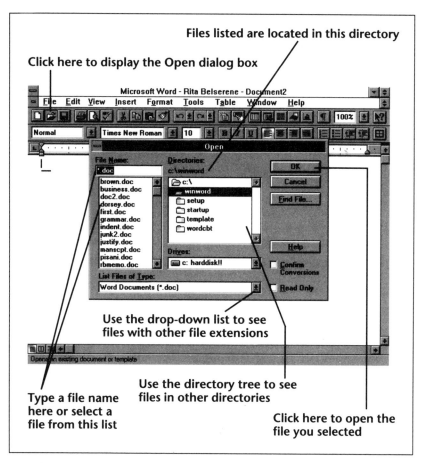

Use the drop-down list to see
files with other file extensions

Type a file name
here or select a
file from this list

Use the directory tree to see
files in other directories

Click here to open the
file you selected

FIGURE 3.4: *The Open File dialog box*

4

Editing Made Simple

AMONG the most delightful aspects of word processing is the ease with which you can correct mistakes and make changes. In this step, you'll learn simple techniques for editing your work.

• • • Moving the Insertion Point Quickly and Efficiently

The *insertion point* is the blinking vertical line that marks your place in a document. Before you can make editing changes, you need to move the insertion point to the text you want to change.

ACTION *You can move to any part of a document with the four arrow keys (↑, ↓, ←, and →). You can also move to a* **visible** *part of a document by moving the mouse pointer and clicking on the new location.*

Word offers a number of additional techniques for moving the insertion point. These techniques are described below.

Moving the Insertion Point with the Mouse

You can move to any visible part of a document simply by clicking on the new location, but if your document is longer than a few lines you won't be able to see it all at once.

Use *scroll bars* to view other parts a document:

- Use the *vertical* scroll bar on the right side of the document screen to move up and down.
- Use the *horizontal* scroll bar on the bottom of the document window to move back and forth in a wide document.

Figure 4.1 explains how to use the features in the vertical scroll bar. (Techniques for using the horizontal scroll bar are the same.)

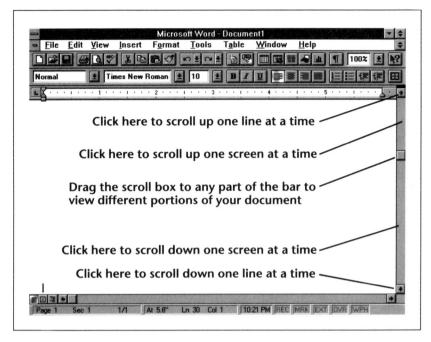

FIGURE 4.1: *Using scroll bars to move around in a document*

Moving the Insertion Point with the Keyboard

You can move the insertion point short distances with the four arrow keys on the keyboard:

- To move the insertion point one character at a time, simply press the appropriate key.

- To move several characters, hold the appropriate key down.

If you've never used a computer before, you may be surprised by how these keys work. For example, when you press → at the end of a line, the insertion point moves to the beginning of the next line. When you press ← from there, the insertion point returns to the end of the previous line.

Word provides a number of techniques for moving the insertion point. These are summarized in Table 4.1.

TO MOVE THE INSERTION POINT	PRESS
Left one word	Ctrl+←
Right one word	Ctrl+→
To the end of a line	End
To the beginning of a line	Home
Up one Paragraph	Ctrl+↑
Down one Paragraph	Ctrl+↓
Up one screen	PgUp
Down one screen	PgDn
To the beginning of a document	Ctrl+Home
To the end of a document	Ctrl+End

TABLE 4.1: *Shortcuts for Moving the Insertion Point*

· · · Adding New Material to a Document

To insert new material in existing text, all you need to do is:

- Move the insertion point where you want to add material and start typing.

For example, to change *man* to *woman*, you would move the insertion point just in front of the *m* and then type *wo*. Existing text is automatically rearranged to make room for the new text.

You can also *type over* existing text. To do this:

1. Either press the *Insert* key or double-click on *OVR* in the status bar to change to *typeover mode.*

2. Start typing. New text replaces existing text as you type.

3. Press the Insert key or double-click on OVR again to return to *insert mode.*

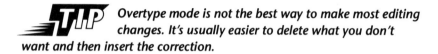 *Overtype mode is not the best way to make most editing changes. It's usually easier to delete what you don't want and then insert the correction.*

• • • Erasing Parts of Your Work

Most editing changes involve erasing work. To delete text one character at a time:

- Press the Delete key to erase the character immediately following the insertion point.

- Press Backspace to erase the character in front of the insertion point.

Shortcuts for deleting blocks of material are summarized in Table 4.2.

• • • Undo and Redo for Correcting Errors

Because few of us are perfect, Word provides two commands to help recover from errors made while editing documents: Undo and Redo. These commands are available on the toolbar and are shown in Figure 4.2.

To undo the last editing change you made:

- Click the Undo button (or press Ctrl+Z).

TO ERASE	USE THIS SHORTCUT
A word	Double-click anywhere on the word and press Delete, or move the insertion point to the beginning of the word and press Ctrl+Delete.
A sentence	Hold down Ctrl and click anywhere in the sentence, and then press Delete.
A line	Click to the left of the line and press Delete.
A paragraph	Triple-click anywhere in the paragraph, and then press Delete.

TABLE 4.2: *Shortcuts for Erasing Text*

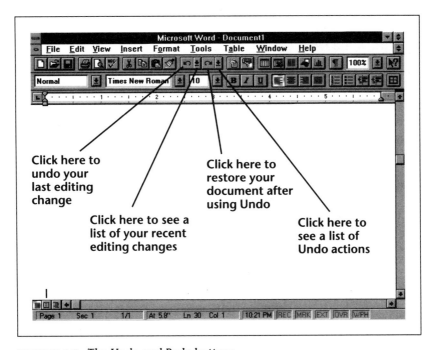

FIGURE 4.2: *The Undo and Redo buttons*

For example, if you just erased a word, you can click Undo to restore it. If you just inserted a word, clicking Undo removes it. You can also use Undo to reverse formatting changes (you'll learn more about formatting in Steps 12 and 13).

 You can click Undo several times to undo your last few actions. You can also see a list of the last several editing changes you've made by clicking the arrow next to the Undo button.

To undo an entire series of actions in one step:

1. Click the arrow to view your recent editing changes.

2. Either click on an item or press ↓ to highlight an item and then press ↵.

To restore your document to the way it was prior to an Undo command:

• Click the Redo button.

 Click the arrow next to the Redo button to restore several Undo actions.

Printing Your Documents

• • • • • • *fast track*

To print the document you're working on,
click the Print button on the toolbar.

To see what a document looks like before you
print it, either click the Print Preview button on
the toolbar or select File ➤ Print Preview.

To print envelopes, select Tools ➤ Envelopes
and Labels. If necessary, click on the Envelope tab.

IN this step, you'll learn how to print documents, how to see
what they look like before you print them, how to work with
the Print dialog box, and how to print envelopes and labels.

••• Printing a Document

The easiest way to print a document is to use the Print button:

1. Open the document you want to print if you have not already done so.

2. Click the Print button on the Standard toolbar (the icon with a picture of a printer).

 *It takes a while for a document to print, but you can keep working with Word while you wait.*

Printing Options

When you want to print several copies of a document or print only part of a long document, use the Print dialog box shown in Figure 5.1. To open the Print dialog box:

- Select File ➤ Print, or
- Press Ctrl+P.

To print several copies of a document:

- Enter a number in the Copies box. You can do this by typing a new value in the box or by clicking on the ↑ or ↓ arrow to increase or decrease the value shown.

To print only the page you are currently working with (the page with the insertion point in it):

- Click Current Page.

To specify one or more pages to print:

1. Click the Pages option.

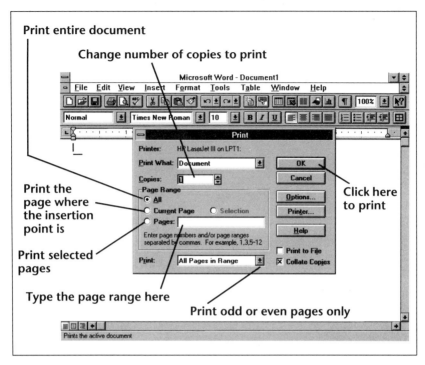

FIGURE 5.1: *The Print dialog box*

2. Tell Word which pages you want printed by entering numbers in the Pages text box.

- To print individual pages, use commas. For example, to print pages 1, 3, and 5, you would enter

  1,3,5

- To print page ranges, use dashes. For example, to print the page range 1 through 5 as well as pages 7 and 9, you would enter

  1-5,7,9

3. Click OK.

• • • Previewing a Document before You Print It

Usually your screen only shows a portion of a page at one time. However, you can "preview" your document to see how it will look when it is printed. Doing this saves time and paper by letting you see if you need to change the page layout before you print the document.

To preview a document:

- Select File ➤ Print Preview, or
- Click the Print Preview button on the toolbar (the button with a piece of paper and a magnifying glass).

The Print Preview screen appears, as in Figure 5.2.

You can use the buttons on the Print Preview toolbar to change the size of the document view:

- The One Page button (see Figure 5.2) displays the view shown in the figure.
- Close returns to the normal document display.

See Figure 5.2 to find out what the other buttons do.

 You can print a document from the Print Preview screen by clicking the Print button in the Print Preview toolbar.

• • • Printing Envelopes

Word makes it easy to print envelopes with correctly positioned addresses. To print an envelope:

- Select Tools ➤ Envelopes and Labels. If necessary, click on the Envelopes tab to see the dialog box shown in Figure 5.3.

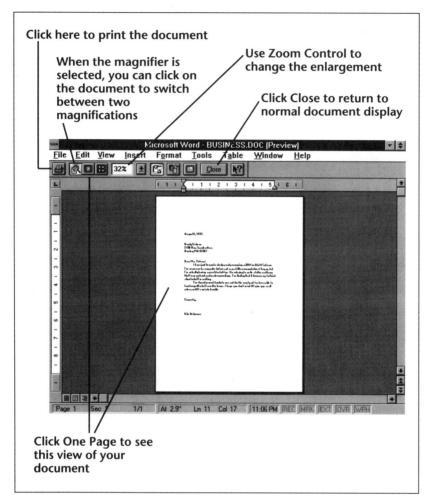

Click here to print the document

When the magnifier is selected, you can click on the document to switch between two magnifications

Use Zoom Control to change the enlargement

Click Close to return to normal document display

Click One Page to see this view of your document

FIGURE 5.2: *Previewing a document*

If you have a letter on screen, Word uses a clever set of rules to determine where the mailing address is, and the program enters this address automatically in the Delivery Address box. However, if there is no address in your document or Word does not successfully display the correct mailing address, type an address into the Delivery Address box.

Word enters an address automatically if there is one
in your document

Use options to select a new envelope size

Click here to print the envelope

Click to omit the return address

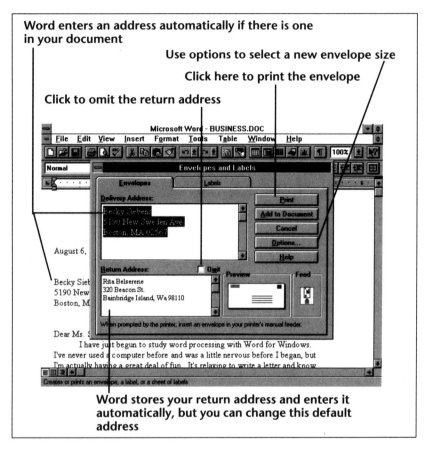

Word stores your return address and enters it
automatically, but you can change this default
address

FIGURE 5.3: *Printing envelopes*

Word stores your return address and enters it automatically in the Return Address box. To change the return address if necessary:

- Type a new address in the Return Address box.

When you type a new address, Word asks you if you want to make it the new default address when you print envelopes. Click OK if you want to store a new default address.

When you are ready to print the envelope:

• Load an envelope in your printer and click Print.

• • • Printing Labels

Word works with a variety of commercially available labels. You can print individual labels, sets of identical labels, or a sheet with different items on each label.

To print labels:

1. Select Tools ➤ Envelopes and Labels.

2. If necessary, click on the Labels tab to display the Envelopes and Labels dialog box in Figure 5.4.

3. To select a label size:

   a. Click the Options button to open the Label Options dialog box.

   b. Scroll through the list under Product Number and highlight your label type on the list. When the label type is highlighted, information about its dimensions and paper size appear under Label Information.

   c. Click OK to select the highlighted label.

If the document you're working with includes a return address, it will be entered automatically under Address in the Labels dialog box.

4. To enter a return address:

• Click Use Return Address to have Word enter your return address (edit your return address by clicking the Envelopes tab and making the changes) or

• Enter the text in the Address text area.

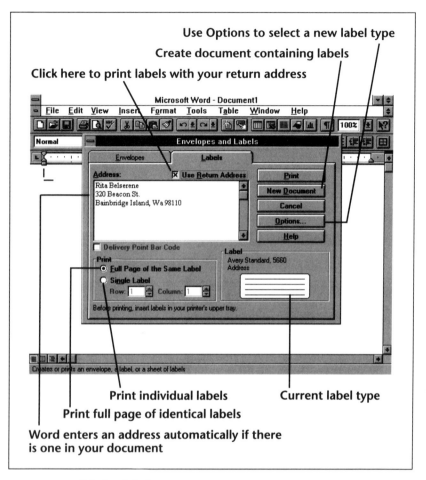

FIGURE 5.4: *Printing labels*

5. You have several options for printing the labels:

- To print an entire page of labels with the address shown, select the Full Page of Same Label option and click Print.

- To print a single label, select the Single Label option, enter a row and column number, and click Print.

- To create a sheet of labels with different items on each label, make sure the Address area is blank and click New Document. A document screen with labels of the size you selected appears. Type a label into each label area. Click in the center of a label area to move to a new label. Save and print this document as you would any other.

6

Selecting and Rearranging Text

• • • • • • *fast track*

To select text, drag the mouse over the text or use one of the shortcuts in Table 6.1.

To select text with the keyboard, hold the Shift key down while you press arrow keys to move the insertion point.

To move text, select the text, click the Cut icon (or press Ctrl+X), move the insertion point to the new location, and click the Paste icon (or press Ctrl+V).

To copy text, select the text, click the Copy icon (or press Ctrl+C), move the insertion point where you want to insert the copy, and click the Paste icon (or press Ctrl+V).

MANY editing tasks involve *selecting*, or highlighting, text. Knowing how to select text efficiently will help you in all your work. In this step, you'll learn how to use your mouse and your keyboard to select text, how to "drag and drop" text, and how to move and copy text with the "cut and paste" method.

• • • Selecting Text to Work With

Figure 6.1 shows a sample document with selected text. You can use your mouse or your keyboard to select text. You must select text before you can delete, copy, or move it.

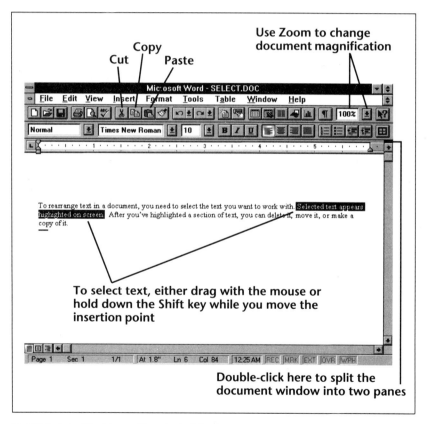

FIGURE 6.1: *Working with selected text*

Selecting Text with the Mouse

One way to select text is to drag the mouse pointer over the text:

1. Move the mouse pointer to the beginning of the text you want to select.

2. Hold the mouse button down while you drag the mouse pointer to the end of the text.

3. Release the mouse button.

> **TIP** *If you highlight text but then decide you don't want to do anything with it, click anywhere in the document window to "unselect" the text.*

Word provides mouse shortcuts for selecting text. These shortcuts are summarized in Table 6.1.

Some text-selection techniques involve using the *selection bar*. The selection bar is the blank area to the left of your text. When the mouse pointer is in the selection bar, it turns into an arrow, as shown in Figure 6.2.

> **TIP** *One quick way to select text is to put the insertion point at the beginning of the text you want to select, then hold down the Shift key while you click at the end of the text you want to select.*

Selecting Text with the Keyboard

To select text with the keyboard:

- Place the insertion point where you want to start selecting text and hold down the Shift key while you move the insertion point.

TO SELECT	USE THIS SHORTCUT
A word	Double-click anywhere in the word
A sentence	Hold down Ctrl and click anywhere in the sentence
A paragraph	Triple-click anywhere in the paragraph *or* double-click in the selection bar next to the paragraph
A line of text	Click in the selection bar next to the line
Several lines of text	Drag in the selection bar next to the lines you want to select
An entire document	Triple-click in the selection bar or press Ctrl and click in the selection bar

TABLE 6.1: *Shortcuts for Selecting Text with the Mouse*

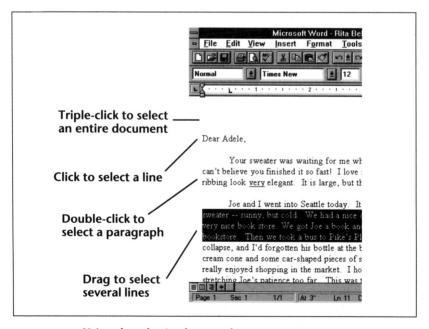

Triple-click to select an entire document

Click to select a line

Double-click to select a paragraph

Drag to select several lines

FIGURE 6.2: *Using the selection bar to select text*

When you select text with the keyboard, you can use a shortcut to move the insertion point. (See Table 4.1 in Step 4 for information about these shortcuts.) To highlight a paragraph, for example, you could place the insertion point at the beginning of the paragraph and press Shift+Ctrl+↓.

To "unselect" text if you decide you do not want to select it:

● Press ↑, ↓, →, or ←. *Do not* press the other keys, because if you do your selected text will be deleted and be replaced by the character whose key you pressed.

● Click outside the selected text.

A quick way to select an entire document is to press Ctrl+A.

• • • Deleting and Replacing Text

To delete text:

1. Select it with mouse or keyboard.

2. Press either the Delete or the Backspace key.

To replace highlighted text:

1. Highlight the text.

2. Begin typing. The text you type replaces the highlighted text.

Anything you type while text is selected replaces the selected text. If you replace text accidentally, restore it by Pressing the Undo button.

• • • Moving Text to a New Location

There are two ways to move text to a new location. You can use a "drag and drop" or a "cut and paste" approach.

 If you make errors moving text, you can restore your document to the way it was before with the Undo button.

The "Drag and Drop" Method of Moving Text

The easiest way to move text short distances is to drag it from one part of the screen to another:

1. Select the text you want to move.

2. Move the mouse pointer to any part of the highlighted text.

3. Click and hold the mouse button. A square appears below the mouse-pointer arrow, as shown in Figure 6.3.

4. Move the mouse pointer where you want to move the text and release the mouse button.

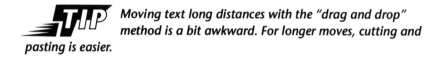 Moving text long distances with the "drag and drop" method is a bit awkward. For longer moves, cutting and pasting is easier.

The "Cut and Paste" Method of Moving Text

Another way to move text is to *cut* it from one location and *paste* it in another. You can cut and paste with the buttons in the toolbar, shortcut keys, or the Cut and Paste commands on the Edit menu.

To move text using Cut and Paste commands:

1. Select the text you want to move.

2. To give the Cut command use one of these techniques:

- Click the Cut button on the toolbar.
- Press Ctrl+X.
- Select Edit ➤ Cut.

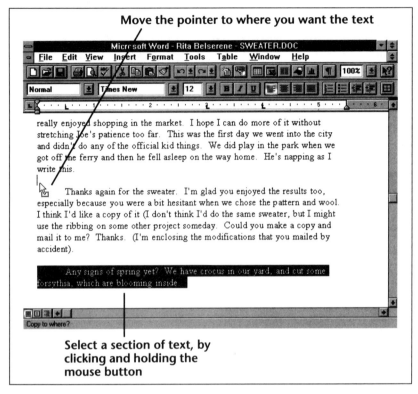

FIGURE 6.3: *The "drag and drop" method of moving text*

The selected text disappears.

3. Move the insertion point where you want the text to be.

4. Paste the text in, using one of these techniques:

- Click Paste on the toolbar.
- Press Ctrl+V.
- Choose Edit ➤ Paste.

The text reappears in the new location.

Text you remove with the Cut command is stored in the *Clipboard*. It remains there until you use the Cut or Copy command again and the new text you cut or copy replaces what was there before. You can place the text in the Clipboard into your document as many times as you want by giving the Paste command.

NOTE *When you remove highlighted text by pressing the Delete key, the text is not stored in the Clipboard and does not replace text that is stored there.*

• • • Copying Text

To make a copy of text and place it to a new location:

1. Select the text you want to copy.

2. Make a copy of the text using one of these techniques:

- Click Copy on the toolbar.
- Press Ctrl+C.
- Select Edit ➤ Copy.

The text remains highlighted.

3. Move the insertion point where you want to insert the copy.

4. Insert the copied text using one of these techniques:

- Click Paste on the toolbar.
- Press Ctrl+V.
- Select Edit ➤ Paste.

A copy of the text appears in the new location.

When you use the Copy command, a copy of the text is placed on the Clipboard. It will remain there until you replace it by cutting or copying new text. You can make copies of the text in the Clipboard as many times as you want.

You can copy text from one document to another. See Step 18 for information about working with several documents at a time.

Getting On-Line Help

•••••• **fast track**

Press F1, or use the Help menu to activate Help.

To open a new Help window, click on any underlined term in a Help window.

To see the definition of a term with dotted underlining in a Help window, click on the term (when the pointer changes to a hand).

To work on your document without closing Help, click outside the Help window. Press Alt+Tab to redisplay the Help window.

FOR those times when you need help with using Word's many features, this step explains how to navigate and use Word's on-line Help system.

··· The Help Windows

Word displays Help information in two kinds of windows:

- The main Help windows provide general reference information and help you locate Procedure windows.

- *Procedure* windows (identified by the words *How To* in the title bar) give step-by-step instructions for using Word features.

Figure 7.1 shows both kinds of Help windows. Key features of these windows are identified in the figure.

TIP *Click outside an open Help window to put your document window "on top" of the Help window and view your document. To put an open Help window back on top, press Alt+Tab.*

··· Searching for Topics You Need Help With

The Search feature is usually the quickest way to look up Help topics. To use this feature:

1. Select Help ➤ Search for Help On or click the Search button in a Help window. The Search window appears.

2. Type a word describing the topic you need help with. The program will display an indexed list of features.

3. Click on an item in the list.

4. Click on Show Topics. This displays a list of related topics.

5. Click on a topic.

6. Click on Go To to open the Help window for that topic.

Click here to print the contents of a procedure window

Double-click here to close a Help window

Click here to see your previous Help selection

Click here to see a list of Help windows you have viewed

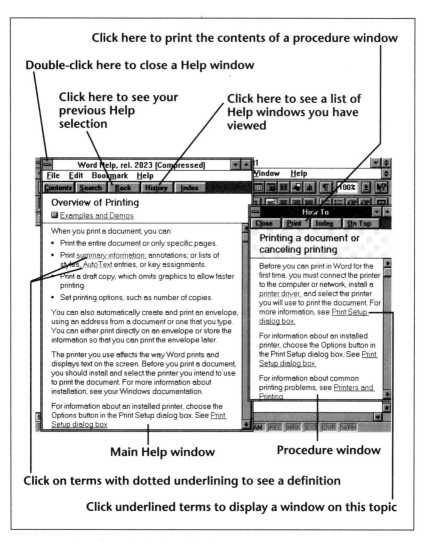

Main Help window

Procedure window

Click on terms with dotted underlining to see a definition

Click underlined terms to display a window on this topic

FIGURE 7.1: *Working with Help windows*

• • • The On-Line Table of Contents

The Help system includes an on-line table of contents with a short list of general subject areas. To get help with a specific subject, use one of these techniques:

- Select Help ➤ Contents.
- Press F1 (make sure no menus or dialog boxes are open).
- Click the Contents button in a main Help window.

> *TIP* *To get help concerning a dialog box, press F1 when the dialog box is open. To get information concerning a menu command, open the menu, highlight the command, and then press F1.*

• • • Using the Help Index

The on-line index lists Help topics alphabetically. You can look up a subject you need help with in the index:

1. Select Help ➤ Index or click the Index button in any Help window.

2. Click on a letter button to jump to that part of the alphabet. Use the scroll bars in the Help window to browse through this portion of the index.

3. Click on an item to open a Help window on that topic.

• • • Tutorials for Using Microsoft Word

The tutorial features in the Help system provide demonstrations and step-by-step assistance for working with Word. To see an example or a demonstration:

1. Select Help ➤ Examples and Demos.

2. Click on a button to see a demonstration of the topic you are interested in.

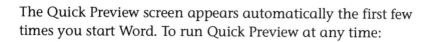

The Quick Preview screen appears automatically the first few times you start Word. To run Quick Preview at any time:

1. Select Help ➤ Quick Preview.

2. Click on a button to select a Quick Preview topic.

8

Using Find and Replace

•••••• *fast track*

To find a word in a document, select Edit ➤ Find (or press Ctrl+F), type the word in the Find What text box, and click Find Next.

To replace text, select Edit ➤ Replace (or press Ctrl+H), type the text you want to replace in the Find What text box, and type the text you want to replace it with in the Replace With text box. Click the Find Next button to find the text and then click Replace if you want to replace it, or click Replace All to replace all instances of the text without reviewing them one at a time.

MANY editing tasks can be done faster and easier by using Word's find and replace features. In this step, you will learn how to search for text in a document, and how to find one item and replace it with another.

• • • Finding Text

To find a word or phrase in a document:

1. Select Edit ➤ Find (or press Ctrl+F). The Find dialog box shown in Figure 8.1 appears.

2. Type the word (or phrase) you want to find in the Find What text box.

3. Click Find Next.

 *See "Controlling the Search" at the end of this Step for information about the various search options you have.*

The Find dialog box remains open and Word moves to the next occurrence of text you are searching for. The text you are looking for is highlighted in your document.

4. At this point you can end the search or look for the next occurrence of the text:

- Click Find Next again to search for the next occurrence.

- Click Cancel to close the dialog box and end the search.

When Word has completed its search through your document, or if a match can't be found, a dialog box appears to tell you so.

5. Click OK to close the dialog box.

• • • Finding and Replacing Text

You can use Word's Replace command to replace a word or phrase with a new one. For example, if you were writing a company report about O'Hara Fumigation and the company

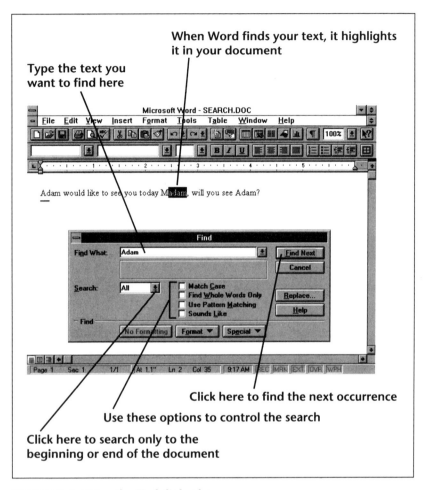

When Word finds your text, it highlights it in your document

Type the text you want to find here

Click here to find the next occurrence

Use these options to control the search

Click here to search only to the beginning or end of the document

FIGURE 8.1: *Using the Find dialog box*

suddenly changed its name to Clean Environments, Inc., you could find and replace the old company name quickly.

To find and replace a word or phrase:

1. Select Edit ➤ Replace or press Ctrl+H. The Replace dialog box shown in Figure 8.2 appears.

2. Type the word or phrase you want to replace in the Find
What text box.

3. Type the text you want to replace it with in the Replace
With text box.

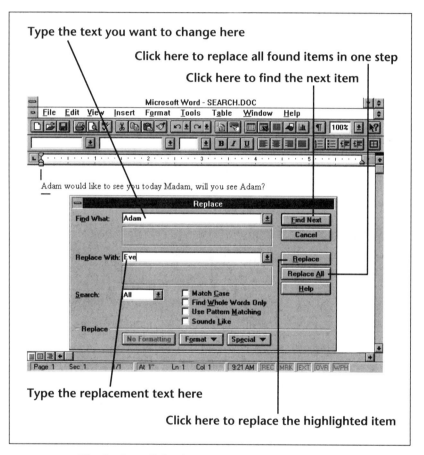

Type the text you want to change here

Click here to replace all found items in one step

Click here to find the next item

Type the replacement text here

Click here to replace the highlighted item

FIGURE 8.2: *The Replace dialog box*

NOTE See *"Controlling the Search"* at the end of this Step to learn about the different options you have for telling Word what to search for.

You can replace all instances of the word or phrase at once or you can review each instance and decide whether or not you really want to replace it.

To replace all instances of the word or phrase:

- Click Replace All.

WARNING *The Replace All option can produce unexpected results. For example, if you replace* man *with* person, *all instances of the word* manage *will change to* personage. *After you perform a Replace All operation, check to see that text was replaced correctly. If it wasn't, use Undo to put the original text back in the document, and start all over.*

To decide item by item whether or not to replace the text:

1. Click the Find Next button (after you have filled in the Find and Replace With text boxes). Word will highlight the first instance of the word or phrase you are looking for.

2. Either replace the highlighted text or continue the search without changing the highlighted word:

- Click Replace to replace the text and continue the search.
- Click Find Next to let the word or phrase stand and keep searching.

· · · **Controlling the Search**

Both the Find and Replace dialog boxes have four check boxes
at the bottom for determining how Word conducts a search:

CHECK BOX	PURPOSE
Match Case	Finds text that matches the capitalization of the text in the Find What box. For example, if you were looking for the name Thomas Brown in a document but you didn't want the program to stop on the word *brown*, you would enter *Brown* in the Find What text box and check the Match Case option.
Find Whole Words Only	Finds specific words, not words within words. For example, checking this option if you were looking for the word *man* would keep the program from stopping on the words *manage* and *talisman*.
Use Pattern Matching	Lets you conduct searches with *wildcard characters* (see below).
Sounds Like	Lets you search for words that have the same pronunciation but different spellings. For example, you could search for *theater* and *theatre*, or *Karl* and *Carl*.

A wildcard character is an unspecified character or group
of characters. Use wildcards in searches when you are not sure
of the spelling of a word. There are two wildcard characters:

* An asterisk. Include an asterisk in the Find What
text to represent one or more unspecified
characters. For example, entering *p*t* in the Find
What text box would find the words *pot, plot,* and
pilot.

? A question mark. Include a question mark to represent a single unspecified character. For example, entering *p?t* would find *pot* and *put*, but not *plot* and *pilot*.

Correcting
Misspelled Words

IN this step, you'll learn how to take advantage of one of the greatest inventions known to typists—the spell checker. This step also explains how to find out how to spell a word.

··· Running the Spell Checker

You can use Word's spell checker

- To locate and correct misspelled words
- To locate and correct duplicate words

Word will not only find your misspelled words, it will—in most instances—provide you with a list of correctly spelled alternatives.

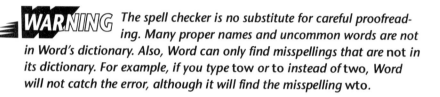 *The spell checker is no substitute for careful proofreading. Many proper names and uncommon words are not in Word's dictionary. Also, Word can only find misspellings that are not in its dictionary. For example, if you type* tow *or* to *instead of* two, *Word will not catch the error, although it will find the misspelling* wto.

Getting Started

To check spelling, you'll use the Spelling dialog box shown in Figure 9.1. In the figure, a spell check is in progress, and an error in the document has been found.

To begin a spell check, use one of these techniques to open the Spelling dialog box:

- Select Tools ➤ Spelling.
- Click the Spelling icon in the toolbar (see Figure 9.1).
- Press F7.

Word will check the entire document regardless of where the insertion point was when you opened the dialog box.

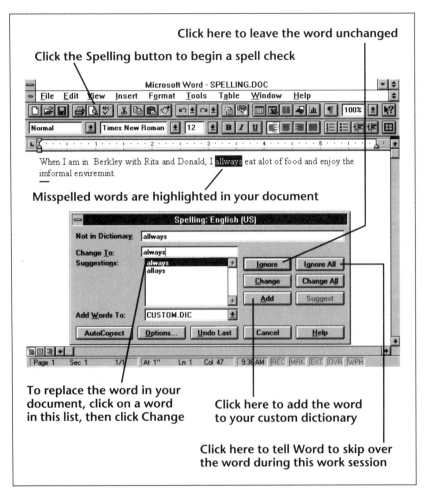

FIGURE 9.1: *Using the Spelling dialog box*

Choosing an Alternative Word

When the program encounters a word that is not in its built-in dictionary, it highlights that word and displays it in the Not in Dictionary area of the Spelling dialog box. The program also displays a list of alternative words in the Suggestions area. To

replace an incorrect word in your document with a word in
the Suggestions list:

1. Click on the correct word if it is not already in the
Change To box.

2. Click Change.

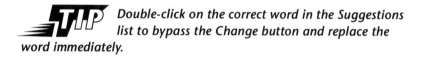 Double-click on the correct word in the Suggestions
list to bypass the Change button and replace the
word immediately.

Letting Misspelled Words Remain Unchanged

If you want an apparent misspelling to remain unchanged:

- Click Ignore to skip over the word in this instance,

- Click Ignore All to skip over the word throughout the
document, or

- Click Add to add the word to your own custom dictionary.
Once a word is added this way, the program will consider
it a correctly spelled word and will not stop on it in future
spell checks.

*If you choose the Ignore All option, the program will ig-
nore the apparent misspelling not only throughout the
document, but throughout the current work session. (A work session ends
when you quit Word.)*

Fixing Misspelled Words Yourself

Some misspellings—for example, *alot* instead of *a lot*—must
be corrected manually. When the program stops on a word
like this:

1. Edit the word in the Change To text box.

2. Click Change.

... Finding Out How to Spell a Word

Inevitably, Word cannot suggest corrections for some misspellings (such as *enviremint for environment*). When the program finds a misspelled word and cannot suggest a replacement, and you do not know the correct spelling yourself, you can use the Change To text box in the Spell dialog box to look up word spellings.

To find the correct spelling of a word:

1. In the Change To text box, type only the parts of the word you are sure of, and enter an asterisk (*) for the parts of the word you are unsure of. In our example, you could type *env*nt* to look up the correct spelling of *environment*.

2. Click Suggest to see a list of words that fit this pattern.

3. Double-click on the correct spelling, if Word displays it, to insert the correct word in your document.

10

Using the Thesaurus

●●●●●● *fast track*

To find a word synonym and place it in a document, choose Tools ➤ Thesaurus or press Shift+F7, highlight the word you want, and click Replace.

To make the thesaurus display more synonyms, highlight a word in the Replace with Synonym list and click Look Up.

If you've displayed more than one synonym list and you want to see a list you saw earlier, click on the Previous button.

BESIDES the spell checker (covered in Step 9), Word offers another valuable writing tool—the thesaurus.

... **Finding Synonyms with the Thesaurus**

You can use Word's thesaurus to find word synonyms. A *synonym* is a word that has the same or nearly the same meaning as another word. The thesaurus can be very useful when you are writing and can't seem to find the right word.

To find a synonym for a word in your document:

1. Place the insertion point anywhere in the word.

2. Open the Thesaurus dialog box shown in Figure 10.1:

- Select Tools ➤ Thesaurus, or
- Press Shift+F7.

The word you selected is highlighted in the document.The Thesaurus dialog box provides the following information:

Looked Up	Displays the word you want to find a synonym for.
Meanings	Displays a list of different meanings and parts of speech for the word you selected. In Figure 10.1, *trial* (a noun) is highlighted, but if you were interested in synonyms for *exam* (a noun similar to *trial*) or *try* (a verb) you could highlight either of these words and make the program display a new set of synonyms in the Replace with Synonyms box.
Replace with Synonym	Lists synonyms for the highlighted word under Meanings.

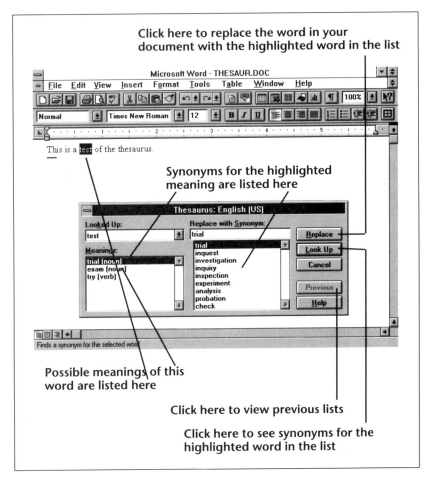

Click here to replace the word in your
document with the highlighted word in the list

Synonyms for the highlighted
meaning are listed here

Possible meanings of this
word are listed here

Click here to view previous lists

Click here to see synonyms for the
highlighted word in the list

FIGURE 10.1: *Working the Thesaurus dialog box*

To see a new list of synonyms:

1. Click on a word in the Replace with Synonym list.

2. Click on the Look Up button.

 *If you've displayed more than one synonym list and you want to go back to a list you saw earlier, click the Previous button.*

To replace the highlighted word in your document with a synonym:

1. Click on a word in the Replace with Synonym list.

2. Click the Replace button.

Working with Fonts

IN this step, you'll learn techniques for working with different lettering styles, or *fonts*. Fonts have three basic characteristics:

- a typeface (for example, Times Roman or Helvetica)

- a font style (for example, boldface or italic)
- a size, known as the *type size*

 **Word also refers to these characteristics as character formatting.**

··· Techniques for Changing Typefaces and Font Size

Figure 11.1 shows the toolbar buttons described in this step. In the figure, the drop-down list of typefaces is displayed.

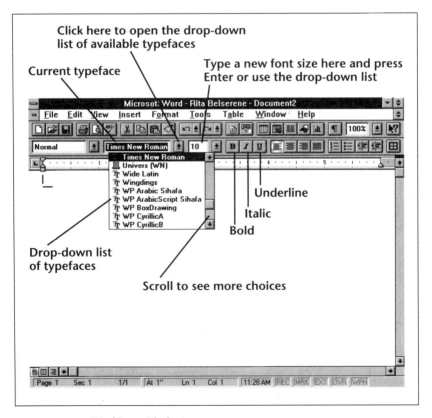

FIGURE 11.1: *Working with fonts*

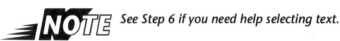 *To determine the font format of a section of text, click the Help button on the toolbar (or press Shift+F1). The mouse pointer will now include a question mark. Using this pointer, click on a text character. Word will open an information box which includes font formatting information. Click the Help button again, or press Esc, when you are done.*

There are two ways to handle typefaces and font size:

- You can change your typeface or font size before you type a section of text. The text will be in the new typeface and font.

- You can change text you have already typed. To do this, select the text you want to change and then change the font. Only the text you selected will be changed.

 See Step 6 if you need help selecting text.

• • • Changing Typefaces

To change typefaces:

1. On the toolbar, click on the ↓ button next to the box that displays the current typeface (see Figure 11.1).

2. Scroll through the list to see which typefaces are available on your system.

3. Click on a typeface name to select that typeface.

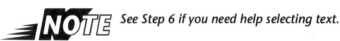 *For your convenience, the typefaces you selected most recently appear at the top of the font list.*

Figure 11.2 shows some examples of different typefaces and different font sizes.

8-point Times New Roman

10-point Courier

14-point Univers

20-point Modern

34-point Arial

42-point Roman

FIGURE 11.2: *Various typefaces and point sizes*

• • • Changing the Size of Text

As Figure 11.2 shows, font size is measured in *points*, with one point equaling $1/72$ of an inch. The point value of a font is the vertical distance from the top of the highest letter to the bottom of the lowest. The number of size choices available depends on the currently selected typeface.

To change font size, use any of these techniques:

• Click on the ↓ button next to the current font size in the toolbar, and click on a new point size.

• Type a new typeface size directly into the box in the toolbar then press Enter. Changing the type size this way allows you to choose sizes that are not listed on the drop-down list.

• Select a section of text and press Ctrl+] to increase the font size by one point, or Ctrl+[to decrease it by one point. Use this technique to change existing text only.

You can change text back to the normal, default font after you have changed the typeface, the point size, or both. To do this, select the text you want to change and press Ctrl+Spacebar.

••• Changing Font Style

To add boldface, italics, or underlining, select the text and use the toolbar buttons labeled in Figure 11.1. You can also use these shortcut keys:

- Press Ctrl+B for **boldface text**.
- Press Ctrl+I for *italic text*.
- Press Ctrl+U for <u>underlining</u>.

If you are adding these attributes as you type, click a toolbar button (or use the shortcut keystroke) before you start typing and click the button again when you are done.

••• Changing the Default Font

Word selects a font for you automatically whenever you open a new document window. This is the *default font*. If you prefer to work with a different font, you do not need to change it each time you open a document.

To change the default font:

1. Select Format ➤ Font. The Font dialog box shown in Figure 11.3 appears.

2. Click on the Font tab if this portion of the dialog box is not already displayed.

3. Use the Font, Font Style, and Size areas to select the attributes you want for your default font.

4. Click the Default button. Word will display a dialog box asking if you want to change to your default font.

4. Click Yes to confirm the change.

The default font will go into effect in your current document and all subsequent documents, but will not alter documents you have already created.

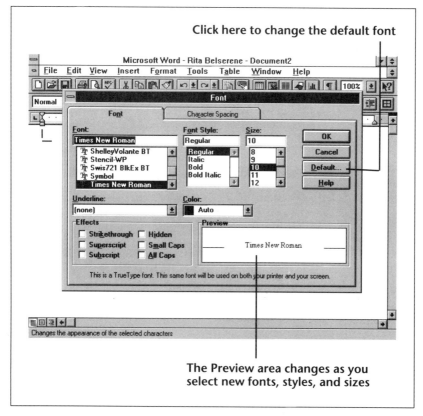

Click here to change the default font

The Preview area changes as you
select new fonts, styles, and sizes

FIGURE 11.3: *The Font dialog box*

Adjusting Margins and Tab Settings

• • • • • • *fast track*

To adjust margins, use Page Layout view and drag the margin boundaries on the horizontal and vertical rulers.

To set tabs, click on the ruler where you want to add a new tab setting.

To adjust the tab settings in existing text, first select the text you want to change.

To set tabs using a new alignment style, click on the Tab Alignment button until you see the symbol for the alignment style you want, and then click on the ruler to set new tabs.

IN this step you'll learn how to adjust page margins, how to change tab settings, and how to work with different tab-alignment styles.

••• Adjusting Margin Settings

Margin settings control the distance between text and the edge of the paper. Normally, Word sets 1-inch margins at the top and bottom of the paper and 1.25-inch margins on the left and right sides. The easiest way to adjust margin settings is with the ruler.

To adjust the margins:

1. Change to the Page Layout view shown in Figure 12.1:

- Click the Page Layout View button on the bottom of the screen (see Figure 12.1), or

- Select View ➤ Page Layout.

In the Page Layout view, the current margin boundaries are shown in gray on the ruler (or in a different color depending on the color scheme you've chosen). To change margin settings:

2. Position the mouse pointer on the margin boundary you want to change. When the pointer is correctly positioned, it will change to a double-arrow.

3. Drag the double-arrow to reposition the margin.

The text in your document, if there is any, will be rearranged when you release the mouse button.

 *If you don't like the margin changes you've made, click the Undo button to return to your previous margin setting.*

To leave Page Layout view and return to the normal document display:

- Click the Normal View button on the bottom of the screen (see Figure 12.1), or

- Select View ➤ Normal.

Drag this boundary to adjust the top margin

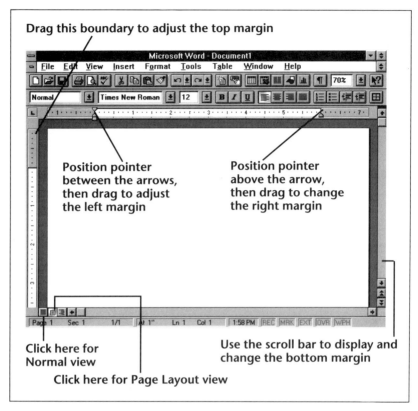

Position pointer between the arrows, then drag to adjust the left margin

Position pointer above the arrow, then drag to change the right margin

Click here for Normal view

Click here for Page Layout view

Use the scroll bar to display and change the bottom margin

FIGURE 12.1: *Adjusting margins with the rulers in Page Layout view*

You can change the default margins settings. To do so, select File ➤ Page Setup and click the Margins tab. Change the margin settings, click Default, and then click Yes. The new settings will affect all subsequent documents you create but not documents you have already created.

• • • Adjusting Tab Settings

When you press the Tab key, the insertion point moves to the next tab stop. By default, tab stops are set at half-inch intervals on the ruler, but you can clear the tabs, add new tab stops, and align text at the tab stops in various ways.

TIP *By displaying the non-printing characters, you can see where tabs have been entered in your document. Tabs are marked with an arrow on screen. To turn the non-printing character display on and off, press the ¶ button on the toolbar.*

How Tabs Affect Documents

In order to work with tab settings, you must understand how tabs affect your document:

- When you make tab changes before you type a document, the new tab settings affect everything you type (until you make subsequent tab changes).

- You can change tab settings for a portion of your document. To do so, select the portion of text whose tab settings you want to change and then change the tabs. The new settings will affect only the selected text.

- If you make tab changes without selecting text first, the changes will affect the current paragraph only (a paragraph ends wherever you press Enter).

Changing and Moving
Tab Settings on the Ruler

Word's default tab stops appear as small gray vertical lines below the ruler. To create your own tab settings:

1. Click on the ruler where you want a new tab setting to be.

A new tab marker (larger than the default markers) will appear on the ruler line, and the default tabs will automatically be cleared up to the position of the tab you just set.

2. Continue to click on the ruler to set additional tabs.

To adjust the tab settings:

- To move a tab, drag it to a new location on the ruler.
- To clear a tab, drag it off the ruler.

··· Left, Center, Right, and Decimal Tab Alignments

As shown in Figure 12.2, Word offers four tab alignment styles:

TAB TYPE	USE
Left	Aligns the left edge of the text at the tab stop (this is the default type).
Center	Centers the text around the tab stop.
Right	Aligns the right edge of the text at the tab stop.
Decimal	Aligns numbers so that the decimal point is at the tab stop.

The four tab types are marked by different symbols on the ruler. These symbols are identified in Figure 12.2.

To set tabs using a new alignment style:

1. Click on the Tab Alignment button (see Figure 12.2). Each time you click on the button, a new tab alignment symbol appears. Continue to click to select the alignment you want.

2. Click on the ruler to set a tab that uses that alignment style.

Click here to select a different
alignment style

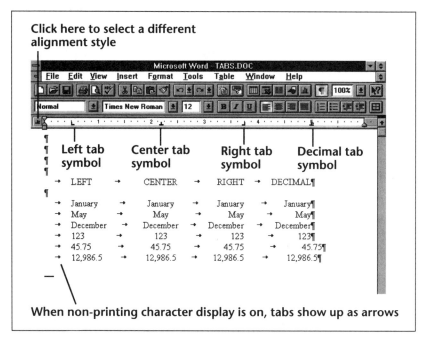

When non-printing character display is on, tabs show up as arrows

FIGURE 12.2: _The four tab alignment styles_

13

Arranging Text on the Page

● ● ● ● ● ● *fast track*

To change the format of a paragraph, place the insertion point in the paragraph and drag the icons on the ruler.

To format several paragraphs, either make formatting changes before you type, or select the paragraphs you want to change before you move the icons on the ruler.

To center, right-align, left-align, or justify text, use the text alignment buttons on the toolbar.

IN Word, you change the format of text by applying format changes to paragraphs. In this step, you'll learn how to indent paragraphs and change line spacing, how to center text and change text justification styles, and how to arrange text in columns.

· · · What You Need to Know to Format Text

As you format text, you need to know what a *paragraph* is in Word:

- A paragraph can be any amount of text. One paragraph ends and the next begins each time you press Enter. Each paragraph ends in a paragraph symbol, which is visible when the non-printing character display is on.

 To turn the non-printing character display on and off, press Ctrl+* (Ctrl+Shift+8).

As you type, Word carries the formatting of the current paragraph on to the next paragraph. So the paragraph formatting you select before you type a document will affect the entire document.

When you change paragraph formatting in a document you have already created, where you place the insertion point is extremely important:

- To change the format of single paragraph, place the insertion point anywhere in a paragraph before changing formats.

- To change the format of several paragraphs at once, select the paragraphs before changing formats.

- To change the format of an entire document, select the entire document. To do this, you can press Ctrl+A; place the mouse pointer in the selection bar on the left side of the screen, hold down the Ctrl key and click once; or triple-click in the selection bar.

WARNING Paragraph formatting is stored with the paragraph symbol (¶) at the end of a paragraph. If you move or copy a paragraph, you must copy the paragraph symbol as well if you want to keep the same formatting.

TIP To determine how an existing section of text is formatted, click the Help button (the question mark) on the toolbar or press Shift+F1. The mouse pointer will change to include a question mark. Click anywhere in a paragraph and Word will open an information box with a Paragraph Formatting area. Click the Help button again or press Esc when you are done.

• • • Indenting Paragraphs

A paragraph *indent* is the amount of space between the paragraph and the left or right margin. As shown in Figure 13.1, Word lets you indent paragraphs in four different ways.

To indent the first line of each paragraph automatically without having to press the Tab key:

- Drag the icon on the ruler (see Figure 13.1) or select Format ➤ Paragraph, click on the Indents and Spacing Tab if necessary, set the Special scroll box to First Line, and enter a number in the By box. The Paragraph dialog box is shown in Figure 13.2.

To indent the left and/or right side of a paragraph (or paragraphs) from the left and/or right margins of the page:

- Drag the appropriate icons on the ruler (see Figure 13.1) or select Format ➤ Paragraph, click on the Indents and Spacing tab if necessary, and enter numbers in the Left and Right boxes.

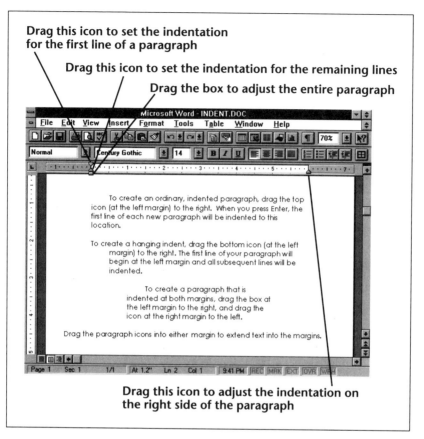

Drag this icon to set the indentation
for the first line of a paragraph

Drag this icon to set the indentation for the remaining lines

Drag the box to adjust the entire paragraph

Drag this icon to adjust the indentation on
the right side of the paragraph

FIGURE 13.1: *Using the ruler to indent paragraphs*

To create *hanging* paragraphs, in which the first line begins
to the left of the rest of the paragraph:

- Drag the bottom icon on the ruler to the right or select
  Format ➤ Paragraph, click on the Indents and Spacing
  tab if necessary, set the Special scroll box to Hanging,
  and enter a number in the By box.

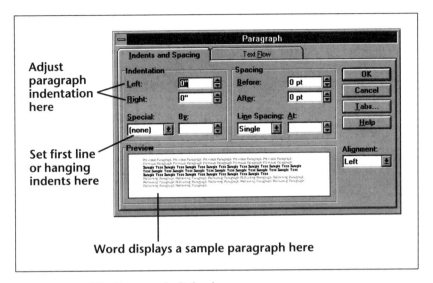

Adjust paragraph indentation here

Set first line or hanging indents here

Word displays a sample paragraph here

FIGURE 13.2: *The Paragraph dialog box*

To extend text into the left and/or right margin:

- Drag the appropriate icons or select Format ➤ Paragraph and enter negative numbers in the Right and Left boxes.

Figure 13.1 explains in detail how to use the ruler icons to format paragraphs. Be sure to place the insertion point in the correct place or select the correct paragraphs before you give a formatting command.

··· Controlling Line Spacing

WARNING *Make sure the insertion point is in the correct place or you've selected the correct paragraphs before you give a line-spacing command.*

You can change line spacing with any of the following techniques:

- Press Ctrl+1 for single spacing.

- Press Ctrl+5 for 1.5-line spacing.
- Press Ctrl+2 for double spacing.

You can also change line spacing with the Paragraph dialog box:

1. Select Format ➤ Paragraph.

2. In the Paragraph dialog box (see Figure 13.2), choose one of Word's line-spacing commands or set the line spacing yourself:

- To choose a Word line-spacing command, click the ↓ in the Line Spacing scroll box and click on the type of line spacing you want.

- To choose a line spacing of your own, click the ↓ in the Line Spacing scroll box and either click Multiple and enter a line spacing number in the At box, or click Exactly and enter a point size value in the At box.

3. Click OK.

⋯ **Centering and Realigning Text**

Word lets you choose from four text alignment styles, as shown in Figure 13.3. By default, Word uses left-aligned text, but you can use toolbar buttons (labeled in the figure) or shortcut keys to select a new alignment style.

WARNING *Make sure you've selected the correct paragraphs or placed the insertion point in the correct paragraph before you give a text alignment command.*

To change the text alignment, use these techniques:

ALIGNMENT	TECHNIQUE
Left-aligned	Press Ctrl+L or click the Align Left toolbar button.

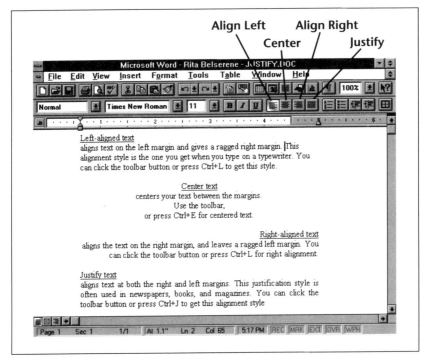

FIGURE 13.3: *Selecting a text alignment style*

ALIGNMENT	TECHNIQUE
Centered text	Press Ctrl+E or click the Center toolbar button.
Right-aligned	Press Ctrl+R or click the Align Right toolbar button.
Justified	Press Ctrl+J or click the Justify toolbar button.

• • • Creating Columns of Text

You can use the Columns button on the toolbar to arrange your text in multiple columns. This button (expanded) is shown in Figure 13.4.

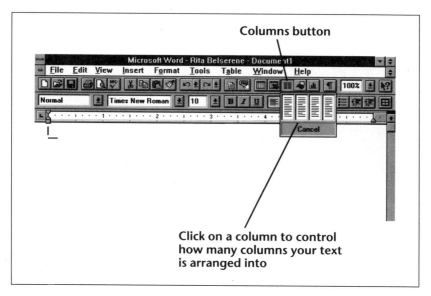

Columns button

Click on a column to control
how many columns your text
is arranged into

FIGURE 13.4: *The Columns button (expanded)*

To create columns of text:

1. Click on the columns button (the icon shows text arranged in two columns). The icon will expand to show you four columns of text.

2. Click in the expanded icon to choose how many columns you want. For example, click on the second column if you want two columns of text.

Columns appear side-by-side in Page Layout view. In Normal view, each column appears beneath the previous one.

To change a document with multiple columns into a normal, single-columns document, click on the first column in the expanded icon.

In Page Layout view, you can use the ruler to adjust column width and the distance between columns. Select View ➤ Page Layout to see Page Layout view.

14

Page Numbering, Headers, and Footers

• • • • • • *fast track*

To view page formatting features, click the Page Layout button on the bottom of your screen, or select Edit ➤ Page Layout.

To insert page numbers, select Insert ➤ Page Numbers.

To create headers and footers, select View ➤ Header and Footer, enter the text for your header or footer, and click Close.

IN this step you'll learn how to include page numbers in your documents, and also how to create and edit headers and footers. Along with multiple columns (covered at the end of Step 13), page numbers, headers, and footers are considered page format features.

• • • Guidelines for Page Format Features

Follow these guidelines when you work with page format features:

- Page formats can be seen on screen only in Page Layout view. To see this view of a document, either click the Page Layout button on the bottom of your screen or select Edit ➤ Page Layout.

- Page Format commands affect your entire document no matter where the insertion point is when you give a command.

• • • Adding Page Numbers

Word does not automatically number the pages in a document.

To add page numbers to a document and tell Word where to place them on the page:

1. Select Insert ➤ Page Numbers. The Page Numbers dialog box shown in Figure 14.1 appears.

2. Use the Position and Alignment boxes to control where page numbers are placed. The Preview area of the dialog box shows you how your document will look.

3. Click OK.

To remove page numbers from a document:

1. Double-click in the margin that contains your page numbers to open the header and footer editing screen (this screen is described in more detail later in this step).

2. Double-click on the page number to select it (be sure the mouse pointer looks like an I-beam when you do this).

3. Press Delete.

4. Click Close to return to the normal editing screen.

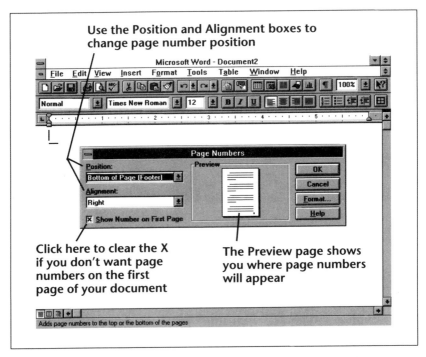

FIGURE 14.1: *Adding page numbers with the Page Numbers dialog box*

· · · Adding Headers and Footers to a Document

Headers and footers are used to display material that is repeated on every page of a document without having to retype the material on each page. *Headers* are printed in the top margin and *footers* are printed in the bottom margin.

To create a header or footer:

1. Select View menu ➤ Header and Footer.

As shown in Figure 14.2, Word will automatically switch to Page Layout view, and an area for creating a header or footer will appear, surrounded by a dashed line. You will also see the Header and Footer toolbar.

2. Enter the text of your header or footer. Use these techniques while you work.

- Switch between headers and footers by using the toolbar button identified in the figure.

- Click the Page Number button if you want to include page numbers in your header or footer.

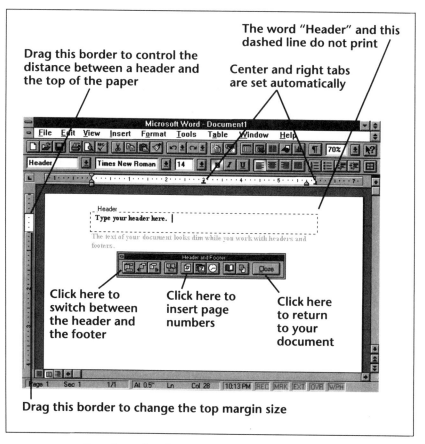

FIGURE 14.2: *Creating a header*

- Press the Tab key once before you type if you want a centered header or footer. Press Tab twice for right-aligned text.

3. Click the Close button, or double-click in the document area of your screen.

To edit a header or footer:

1. View your document using the Page Layout view. Do this by selecting View ➤ Page Layout.

2. Double-click in the area of the screen that contains the header or footer you want to edit.

3. Edit the text, then double-click in the document area of your screen.

To delete a header or footer:

1. Select View ➤ Header and Footer.

2. Select the header or footer you want to delete.

3. Press Delete.

4. Click the Close button, or double-click in the document area of your screen.

Working with Styles

WHEN you are creating and formatting documents, styles can be very useful. Understanding how to work with styles saves time and helps you work more efficiently. By using styles, you can create consistent, professional-looking documents. In this step you'll learn what a style is and some basic techniques for working with styles.

··· What Is a Style?

A *style* is a group of formatting commands that have been given a name and can be applied to different sections of text. For example, a style called "heading" might control font size and typeface. A style called "report" might control line spacing and justification. When you type ordinary text in a document, you are using a style called *Normal*. This is one of many styles that Word has already created and defined for you.

Rules for Working with Styles

As you work with styles, keep these rules in mind:

- The style box shows you the name of the current style. This box is shown in Figure 15.1. New text you type will use this style.

- There are two kinds of styles, paragraph and character. *Paragraph* styles affect whole paragraphs and can include both character and paragraph formatting features. In the style box, paragraph styles are shown in boldface text (see Figure 15.1). *Character* styles affect one or more characters and can only include character formatting. In the style box, character styles are not bold (see Figure 15.1).

- When you modify a style, other text in the same document that you created with that style will be changed.

- Word provides many built-in styles. You can select new styles by using the style box in the toolbar. You can change the list of available styles by changing *templates.*

NOTE *A template is a preformatted document with predefined styles you can apply to new documents. Word provides a number of templates for documents such as memos, letters, resumes, and much more. Templates are covered in Step 16.*

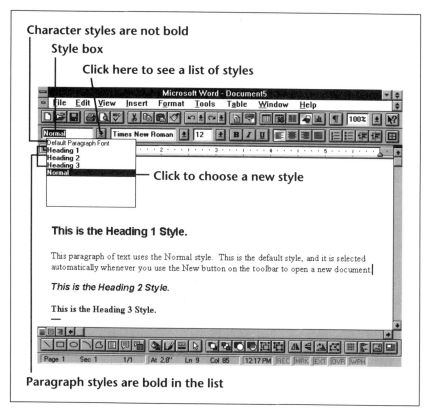

Character styles are not bold

Style box

Click here to see a list of styles

Click to choose a new style

Paragraph styles are bold in the list

FIGURE 15.1: *Styles available in the Normal template*

The Normal Template

Documents are automatically set to use the Normal template when you first create them. The Normal template offers a small number of built-in styles, as shown in Figure 15.1. The sample text in the figure was created with these styles.

• • • Selecting a New Style

When you select a new style, be careful where you place the insertion point. Where you place the insertion point tells Word how much text you want to apply the new style to.

To change styles before you type:

- Begin with a clear screen or place the insertion point at the end of any existing text. The style you select will affect the text you type next.

To change the style of a specific paragraph:

- Place the insertion point in the paragraph before choosing a new *paragraph* style. The entire paragraph will be formatted using the new style.

To change the style of a word:

- Place the insertion point in the word before choosing a new *character* style. The new style will affect just the word at the insertion point.

To change the style of a selection of text:

- Select the text before choosing a new style. If you choose a *paragraph* style, all paragraphs in the text you selected will be given the new style, no matter whether you selected all or part of a paragraph. However, if you choose a *character* style, only the selected text—not the whole paragraph—will change.

To select a new style using the toolbar style box:

1. Place the insertion point in the text, or select the text whose style you want to change.

2. Click on the ↓ next to the style box (see Figure 15.1).

3. Click on the name of the style you want.

••• Adding a New Style to the Style List

You can create new paragraph styles from your own text:

1. Select one or more paragraphs of text.

2. Format the text using the formatting features you want for the new style.

3. Click in the style box in the toolbar.

4. Type a name for the new style and press Enter. (The style name that was there will disappear from the style box, but will remain available in the list you see when you click the ↓.)

You can now apply this style to new sections of text just as you would any built-in style. Styles you create this way are saved as part of the current document. They do not appear on the list of styles when you open a new document with the Normal template.

NOTE *If you want to use your styles in other documents you work with, you may want to create your own templates. Refer to on-line Help for information about creating new templates and modifying existing ones.*

••• Changing Styles throughout a Document

Suppose you've applied a certain style to all the paragraphs or headings in a document, but after printing the document you decide you don't like the style after all. Word lets you change styles throughout a document. You don't have to reformat each section of text individually.

To change styles throughout a document:

1. Select a section of text that you formatted using the style you want to change.

2. Make the formatting changes you want to the selected text. For example, you could change the typeface or font size.

3. Click the style box and press Enter.

4. Click OK in the box that opens.

When you are done, all sections of text you created with the original style will change to the new style.

Shortcuts for Formatting Documents

• • • • • • *fast track*

To use a Wizard, select File ➤ New, highlight the name of the Wizard you want to work with, and click OK.

To use a template, open the File menu, select New, highlight the name of the template you want to work with, and click OK.

To have AutoFormat format a document you have already typed, open the Format menu and select AutoFormat. Word will display a proposed format for your work. Click Accept to accept the changes.

WORD offers a number of shortcuts for formatting documents. This step explains Wizards, templates, and automatic formatting. With these features, you can create professional-looking documents quickly. Using the formatting shortcuts described in this step may also give you ideas for formatting and designing your own documents.

• • • Predesigned Wizard Documents

A *Wizard* is a preformatted document created by Word. By using Wizards, you can create a broad range of documents, including business letters, memos, resumes, newsletters, and tables.

To use a Wizard:

1. Select File ➤ New. A list of templates and Wizards appears. (Wizards include the word *Wizard* in their name.)

2. Highlight the name of the Wizard you want to work with.

 By highlighting Wizards on the list, you can see a brief description of each one in the Description area of the box.

3. Click OK to work with the highlighted Wizard.

In a moment, a Wizard box appears. Figure 16.1 shows the Award Wizard box.

4. Click a style option for your document.

5. Click Next to move on to the next step.

6. Follow the on-screen directions. Click Next when you are done with each step. Click Back to make changes to the work you've already done.

7. Click Finish when you are done.

Word will create a document using the formatting and text information you supplied. You can edit, save, and print this document as you would any other.

• • • Working with Templates

A *template* provides a formatting framework you can use to create a document. As with Wizards, templates are available for creating a broad range of documents.

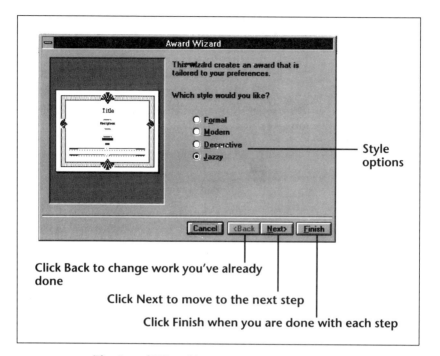

FIGURE 16.1: *The Award Wizard box*

To use a template:

1. Select File ➤ New.

2. Highlight the name of the template you want to work with and click OK.

Word will open a document with the template you selected.

Figure 16.2 shows a sample template (called Letter1) that you might use to create a business letter. The task of formatting the document and creating styles is already done for you. Notice the instructions and generic entries in brackets. Delete these entries and replace them with text of your own. Save and print the document as you would any other.

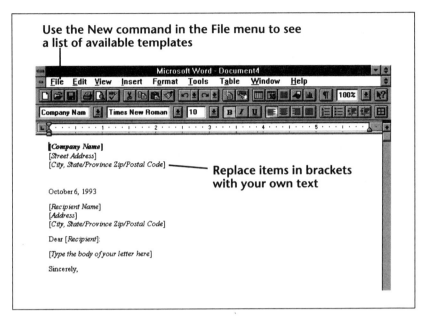

Use the New command in the File menu to see a list of available templates

Replace items in brackets with your own text

FIGURE 16.2: *Using a template to create a business letter*

••• Using AutoFormat

Word can also format documents automatically after you type them. Word will automatically recognize key text elements—such as headings and bulleted lists—and use this information to enhance your document's layout. Word shows you the changes it proposes before making them, so it is easy to experiment with the AutoFormat feature.

To format a document automatically:

1. Place the insertion point anywhere in the document.

2. Select Format ➤ AutoFormat.

3. Click OK.

4. Word displays a proposed format for your work. Scroll through your document to view these formatting changes.

5. You can accept all the changes, reject them all, or accept them on a change-by-change basis:

- Click Accept to accept all changes.
- Click Reject All to leave your document as it was.
- Click Review Changes to accept or reject individual changes.

 *See on-line Help for more information about the Review Changes option.*

Adding Visual Appeal to Documents

●●●●●● *fast   track*

To create bulleted or numbered lists, use the Numbering or the Bullets button on the toolbar.

To add borders to a paragraph, select Format ➤ Borders and Shading, use the Borders tab to select a border style, and click OK.

To add a picture to a document, select Insert ➤ Picture, click on the file name of the picture you want, and click OK.

FIGURE 17.1 demonstrates a number of different elements you can use to add visual appeal to a document. In this step, you'll learn techniques for creating numbered and bulleted lists, creating borders, and adding graphic pictures to documents.

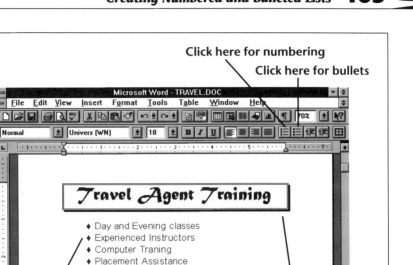

FIGURE 17.1: *A document with a border, a bulleted list, and a graphic image.*

 To avoid creating busy, cluttered pages, limit the number of visual elements you place on a page.

• • • Creating Numbered and Bulleted Lists

Creating a numbered or bulleted list is easy with Word. To create these lists, use the Numbering and Bullets buttons in the toolbar (see Figure 17.1.)

To add bullets (or numbers) as you type:

1. Click the Bullets (or Numbering) button. You'll see a bullet (or number) appear at the beginning of the line.

2. Type your list, pressing Enter after each item. New bullets (or numbers) appear automatically.

3. Press Enter after you type your last item.

4. Click the Bullets (or Numbering) button again to remove the unneeded bullet (or number) on the last line and return to normal typing.

To add bullets or numbers to a list you've already typed:

1. Select the list.

2. Click the Bullets or the Numbering button.

You can also change the appearance of existing bulleted or numbered lists:

• You can select different bullets for a bulleted list.

• You select a new numbering or lettering style.

• You can change bullets to numbers or numbers to bullets.

To make any of these changes:

1. Select the list you want to change.

2. Select Format ➤ Bullets and Numbering.

3. Select a new bulleting, numbering, or lettering style by referring to the samples shown in the dialog box.

4. Click OK.

TIP *When you use the Bullets and Numbering dialog box to change the bullet or numbering style, Word will use the new style for the next list you create as well as the currently selected list.*

• • • Creating Borders

You can place borders around individual paragraphs or groups of paragraphs. (Remember that a paragraph is any amount of text ending with an Enter.)

To place a border around a paragraph:

1. Place the insertion point anywhere in the paragraph.

2. Select Format ➤ Borders and Shading. If necessary, click on the Borders tab.

3. Select the border style that you want by clicking on one of the samples.

4. Click either Box or Shadow. You'll see a preview of the border style you've selected.

5. Click OK.

To add a border to several paragraphs:

1. Select the paragraphs.

2. Follow steps 2 through 5 above.

To remove a border:

1. Place the insertion point anywhere within the border.

2. Select Format ➤ Borders and Shading. If necessary, click on the Borders tab.

3. Click the picture labeled None.

4. Click OK.

• • • **Adding Pictures to Your Work**

Word supplies you with a number of pictures that you can add to your documents. To insert one of these pictures:

1. Select Insert ➤ Picture.

2. Scroll through the list of picture file names. You can click on a name to preview the picture and see what it looks like.

3. Click OK.

NOTE When you add a picture to an existing section of text, Word places it at the insertion point location and arranges the text above and below the picture. If you want to have more control over how a graphic image is positioned in your document, you need to add a **frame** to your picture. See on-line Help for information about using frames. You can also use frames to place borders around pictures.

To change the size of a picture:

1. Click on the picture to select it. When a graphic image is selected, square *sizing handles* appear on the corners and sides, as shown in Figure 17.2.

2. Drag the sizing handles to change the picture size.

3. Click outside the picture when you are done.

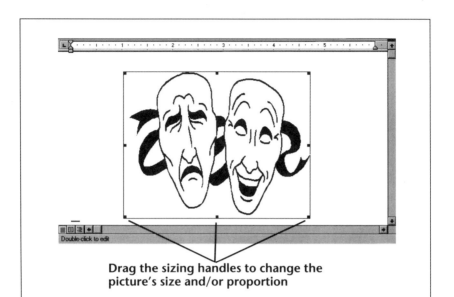

Drag the sizing handles to change the
picture's size and/or proportion

FIGURE 17.2: *An enlarged picture*

18

Working with Several Documents at Once

● ● ● ● ● ● *fast track*

To open a new document without closing the one(s) you are working with, click the New button in the toolbar.

To switch between documents, either press Ctrl+F6 to cycle through them, or open the Window menu and click on the document you want to view.

To copy or move text from one document to another, select the text in the current document, click Copy or Cut on the toolbar, switch documents, place the insertion point in the new document where you want to insert the text, and then click Paste.

IN this step you'll learn editing techniques that involve using more than one document. You'll also learn how to control the way multiple documents are displayed on screen.

··· Opening Several Documents at a Time

When you are working with one document, you can open an existing document without closing the one you are working with. To do this:

- Select File ➤ Open and bring up the document.

The document you open will replace the one you were working with on screen, but both documents will be *active* in your computer's memory, and you can switch easily between them.

To open a new blank document when you have a document open already:

- Click the New button on the toolbar, or
- Select File ➤ New (and select a new template if you wish), then click OK.

Switching between Documents

Use any of these techniques to switch between open documents.

- Open the Window menu and click on the name of the document you want to work with.
- Press Ctrl+F6 to see the next document. Keep pressing Ctrl+F6 to cycle through all open documents.
- Click the document Control button, and choose Next Window. (The Control button you want to use is the one with a small dash immediately to the left of the document's title bar. The Word Control button has a larger dash.)

Copying and Moving Text between Documents

Working with several documents at a time makes it easy to copy or move material from one document to another.

To copy or move text between documents:

1. Place the insertion point in the first document, and select the material you want to copy (or move).

2. Select the Copy (or Cut) command from the Edit menu or the toolbar.

3. Switch to the new document using any of the techniques described above (or open a new blank screen).

4. Position the insertion point where you want the material to go.

5. Select the Paste command by using the Edit menu or the toolbar.

You can insert an entire file into a document on screen. To do this, you don't need to open the file you want to insert. With the document to which you want to add the file on screen, select Insert ➤ File, click on the name of the file you want to insert, then click OK.

Closing Documents
When You're Done with Them

When you have more than one document open at a time, you can close each one individually, or you can let Word close all of them when you exit. To close individual files:

1. Switch to the file you want to close.

2. Select File ➤ Close.

To close all your files and exit from Word:

• Select File ➤ Exit.

If you have already saved all of the open files, Word will close them automatically, but if some files have not been saved, Word displays a dialog box for each unsaved file and asks you if you want to save it.

· · · Working with Windows

By reducing the size of your document windows, you can view several documents at a time. Figure 18.1 shows a sample screen with five open documents, three in small windows and two in icons.

Displaying All Open Documents at Once

To arrange your windows so you can see all of your open documents:

- Select Window ➤ Arrange All.

The Arrange All command automatically arranges windows by reducing each one enough so you can see them all. How the windows are arranged depends on how many documents are open. The more documents that are open, the smaller the windows will be.

Moving and Resizing Windows

You can change both the size and position of a window. To move a window to a new location:

1. Place the mouse pointer anywhere on the window's title bar.

2. Drag the window to its new location.

To change the size of a window:

1. Place the mouse pointer on the narrow border surrounding the window. The pointer changes to a double-pointed arrow.

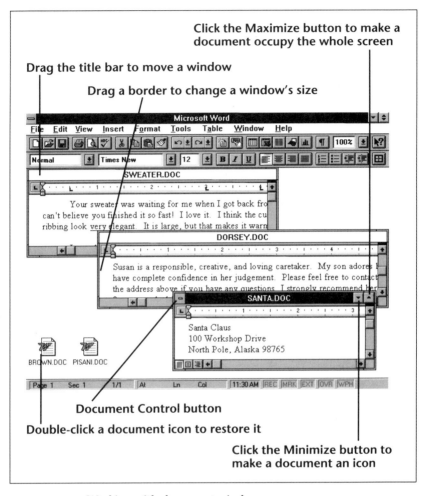

Click the Maximize button to make a
document occupy the whole screen

Drag the title bar to move a window

Drag a border to change a window's size

Document Control button

Double-click a document icon to restore it

Click the Minimize button to
make a document an icon

FIGURE 18.1: *Working with document windows*

2. Drag the border to a new location.

Drag the corner of a window to change its size in two dimensions at once.

Minimizing, Maximizing, and Restoring Windows

To change the display of a document window, use the three basic sizing options: Minimize, Maximize and Restore. All windows have control buttons for "resizing" purposes. Table 18.1 explains the sizing options and shows the Control button symbol associated with the each term.

 *When several visible document windows are on screen, only the sizing buttons on the active window are visible. To make a window the active window, click anywhere on it.*

SYMBOL	TERM	EFFECT
▼	Minimize	Reduces the window to an icon
▲	Maximize	Enlarges the window to fill the screen
▲ ▼	Restore	Displays the window using only a portion of the screen

TABLE 18.1: *Window Sizing Buttons*

To redisplay a document that you have turned into an icon:

1. If necessary, move or resize any open windows so you can see the icons. (Unless you have dragged your icons to a new location, they will be at the bottom of the screen.)

2. Double-click on an icon to restore it to a window.

Organizing Your Files

• • • • • *fast track*

To save files or open files to or from a different directory, use either the Directories area in the Save As or the Open dialog box.

To change the default directory, select Tools ➤ Options, and then select the File Location tab.

To delete or copy files, use the Find File command in the File menu.

IN this step you'll learn techniques for organizing your files into directories. You'll also learn how to delete files.

• • • How Directories Work

Computer files are stored in related groups called *directories*. Directories are like drawers in a file cabinet, in that each stores a different group of related files.

Directories are organized on your disk in a branching fashion, like a tree. At the base of the tree is the *root* directory. It can be divided into branches, or directories, which can in turn be divided into further *subdirectories*.

Directories may contain program files for your software. (Your Word files are most likely installed in a directory called *winword*, which is divided into subdirectories such as *clipart*, *template*, and others.) You can also create your own directories and subdirectories in order to organize your own files.

When you create and save files using Word, they are automatically saved to a directory known as the *default directory*. (If you haven't changed this, it will be the *winword* directory.) Each file you save is identified by a *directory path* as well as a file name. For example, if you type **smith** when you save a file using the *winword* directory, its complete name will be

```
c:\winword\smith.doc
```

Changing Directories

Normally, Word automatically saves files to the *winword* default directory. When you use the Open dialog box to open a file, it will also automatically list the files in the default directory.

To save a file to a different directory:

1. Make sure the file is open and select File ➤ Save As.

2. Double-click on the **C:** at the top of the Directories box to see a list of all the directories that branch off your root directory.

3. Double-click on any directory to save files to that directory. (When you do this, you will also see a list of subdirectories if there are any. Double-click on a subdirectory to save files to it.)

4. Type a name for your file and click OK.

To open files that are stored in a different directory:

1. Select File ➤ Open.

2. Double-click on directories (and subdirectories) in the Directories box to see the files in those directories.

3. Double-click on a file name to open the file.

> **TIP** When you change directories using either Open or Save As, Word continues to use the new directory for opening and saving files until you exit the program or change directories again.

Changing and Creating Default Directories

You may prefer not to mix your document files with the other files in the *winword* directory. You can use any directory on your disk as the default directory, or you can create a new directory to save your files.

To change the default directory that Word uses for saving and opening files:

1. Select Tools ➤ Options, and select the File Locations tab.

2. Click Documents in the File Types list.

3. Click the Modify button to open the Modify Location dialog box. (Use the New button in this box if you want to create a new directory, and type a new directory path in the Name box—for example, *c:\newdirect*—and then click OK.)

4. Type the directory path you want to use for your default directory, or use the Directories box to select a directory.

5. Click OK.

6. Click Close.

• • • Managing Your Files

Keeping your files current and organized can help you work more efficiently. You can maintain your files using the Find File dialog box.

> **NOTE** *Another way to manage your files is with the File Manager, a Windows utility. See your Windows documentation for information.*

Telling Word How to Search for Files

To manage your files, you work with the Find File dialog box. To display this dialog box:

- Select File ➤ Find File.

> **NOTE** *When you use Find File the first time, Word opens the Search dialog box described next. If you have already used this command, Word will automatically open the Find File dialog box using your most recent search options. You can reopen the Search dialog box by clicking the Search button in the Find File dialog box.*

The first time you use the Find File command, you'll see a Search dialog box like the one shown in Figure 19.1. This dialog box determines which files you see listed in the Find File dialog box. Use these key features to control the search:

FEATURE	USE
File Name	Determines which files Word will search for. Enter *.doc to search for all document files with the .doc extension. Enter *.* to search for all files. Enter a specific file to locate that file.

Select which files you want listed here

You'll see this dialog box automatically
the first time you use Find File

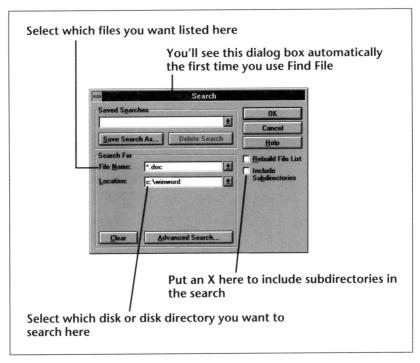

Put an X here to include subdirectories in
the search

Select which disk or disk directory you want to
search here

FIGURE 19.1: *The Search dialog box*

FEATURE	USE
Location	Determines which disk or portion of a disk Word searches through. Enter *c:* (and include subdirectories in your search) to search through your entire hard disk. Enter *c:\winword* (and don't include subdirectories) to list only the files in this directory.
Include Subdirectories	Controls whether or not the search includes subdirectories. When an *X* is present in this box, Word searches all subdirectories of the directory you specified under Location.

Searching for Files to Work With

After you have selected search options in the Search dialog box:

- Click OK to open the Find File dialog box.

Figure 19.2 shows a sample Find File dialog box. In this example, all the document files in the *winword* directory are listed according to the search criteria shown in Figure 19.1. You can use this dialog box for maintaining your files and directories. One of the most frequently used options, deleting files, is described below. Refer to on-line help for information about other file management features.

Deleting Files

To delete a file:

1. Open the Find File dialog box and click once to highlight the file you want to delete.

2. Click the Commands button.

3. Click Delete.

4. Click Yes in the dialog box that opens to confirm that you want to delete the file.

The listed files are determined by the search options you used

The preview area shows the selected file

Click once to select a file (double-click to open one)

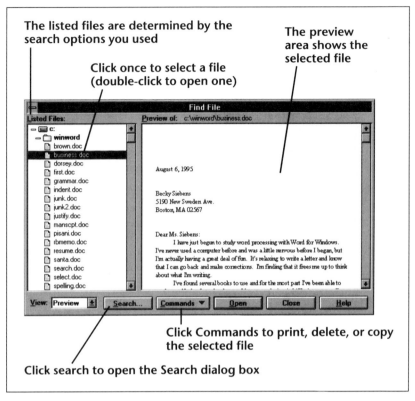

Click Commands to print, delete, or copy the selected file

Click search to open the Search dialog box

FIGURE 19.2: *The Find File dialog box*

Index

Note to the Reader: **Boldface** page numbers indicate definitions and principal discussions of primary topics and subtopics. *Italic* page numbers indicate illustrations.

...... Word Shortcut Keys

Document Shortcuts

Close	Ctrl+W
New	Ctrl+N
Open	Ctrl+O
Print	Ctrl+P
Save	Ctrl+S
Save As	F12

Editing Shortcuts

Copy	Ctrl+C
Cut	Ctrl+X
Delete Word	Ctrl+Del
Find	Ctrl+F
Go To	Ctrl+G
Paste	Ctrl+V
Repeat Typing	Ctrl+Y
Replace	Ctrl+H
Select All	Ctrl+A
Undo	Ctrl+Z

Paragraph Formatting Shortcuts*

Center	Ctrl+E
Double-spacing	Ctrl+2
Hanging indent	Ctrl+T
Indent from Left	Ctrl+M
Justify	Ctrl+J
Left Align	Ctrl+L
Normal Style	Ctrl+Shift+N
Remove formatting	Ctrl+Q